"The Path To Perfection is an exceptionally real representation of parenthood. While reading this journey, it was like I was walking the path with Dawn. It's a book I would recommend to any parent."

Chantelle Lambert, author of "Life as a mother"

The Path to Perfection

The Path to Perfection

*Parenting without a roadmap:
tales from a (non) perfect parent*

DAWN THOMAS-CAMERON

Copyright © 2019 Dawn Thomas-Cameron

All rights reserved. This book or any portion thereof may not be reproduced or used in any manner whatsoever without the express written permission of the publisher except for the use of brief quotations in a book review.

Printed in the United States of America

First Printing, 2019

ISBN: 978-1-64085-519-9 (Paperback)
ISBN: 978-1-64085-520-5 (Hardback)
ISBN: 978-1-64085-521-2 (eBook)

Front cover image by Ronald Cruz, cruzialdesigns
Book design by JetLaunch

Library of Congress Control Number (LCCN): 2018967591

Published by Author Academy Elite
P.O. Box 43, Powell, OH 43035

www.thepathtoperfection.com

This book is dedicated to my late husband, without whom it would never have been written. And to my children who were the inspiration for the book.

Table of Contents

Introduction 1
    The Journey................................. 2
    The Destination............................. 3
    Non-Perfectness 4
    Our Parents................................ 6
    Amazingly We Survived!...................... 7
    Wandering for Hours on End 10
    Normal Dysfunctional 11
    Passing Judgment...........................12
    There Are Children in Other Countries ... .13
    Parents Cry................................14
    Babies Cry.................................15
    Right and Wrong............................17

Part 1 – Things That Could Have Been Done Differently ... 19

- Let Her Cry ... 20
- Tylenol ... 21
- Co-Sleeping ... 21
- Hurry Up! ... 23
- Television IS a Great Babysitter ... 24
- Electronics ARE Great Babysitters ... 24
- Boxes Rule! ... 25
- Why You Should Not Let Your Kids Believe in Santa Claus ... 26
- Call My New Spouse "Mom" or "Dad" ... 29
- Germs ... 29
- Bubble Wrap ... 31
- Just Being Dumb ... 33
- Throwing Teddy Bears ... 33
- Swear Words ... 34
- Candy Shop ... 35
- Discipline ... 35
- Holidays after Divorce or Separation ... 36
- Rules for the Sake of Rules ... 37
- You're Wearing What? ... 42
- Marshmallows versus Brick Walls ... 45
- Play Fighting ... 46
- Dirty Diapers ... 47
- Room Cleaning ... 48
- Temper Tantrums ... 49
- Yelling ... 50
- Child Protective Services ... 51

Apologizing 53
Hair Dye 54

Part 2 – Things I Handled Like a Rock Star! 55

Mirror Obsession 56
Monster Spray 56
Nightmares 58
Playdough Made From Scratch 58
Slime 59
Christmas Presence 60
Family Time 62
Nickelback 63
Washroom Usage 66
Sex Ed 68
Planned Parenthood Classes 68
Sex Ed—New Generation 69
Road Trips 70
Who's Everyone? 75
Grounding Revamped 77
In My Days … 77
Spaced Out Children 79
Ask the Other Parent 80
High School Trip 80
Mama Bear 82
Tattoos 83
Making Responsible Choices 85
Saying No 86
Jobs 87
Social Butterflies 87

Sexual Preferences 88
Young Adults. 89
Easter Egg Hunts 90
Christmas Presents Spy Game 94
Picky Eaters. 95
Gender Norms. 96
    Career Choices 97
    Pink Strollers. 98
    Nail Polish 98
    Girls Can't Be Truck Drivers 99
Paddling Pools 100
Help Me Fix My Car 101
Making Songs Out of Anything 102
    Wheels on the Bus (Semi-exhaustive version) . . .102
    Make up Lyrics 105
    Change up Lyrics. 106
    Rock a Bye Baby 108
Dance Like No One is Watching 109
Grocery Shopping. 109
Can I Have a Bunny?. 110
Hop 111
Calgary Bus Trip 112
Bribing with Broccoli. 113

Part 3 – Pearls of Wisdom 115
Underage Drinking 116
Marijuana 117
Pain. 118
Friend Versus Parent 118

Needles 119
Dealing with Violence 119
Sam and Dean 120
To Flu Shot or Not to Flu Shot 121
Parenting Through Divorce. 123
Divorced Versus Single Parenting. 123
School Marks. 124
The Sanctity of Marriage 126
Contradicting Rules 128
    Stranger Danger. 128
    Unwanted Touching. 129
Babies Having Babies. 130
Pole Dancing. 131
Zombies 132
Bedtime Routines. 133
Turn the Television/Computer Off 135
An Author in Training. 135
Cat to The Rescue 136
Losing J 137
    Our Last Road Trip. 138
    Rapid Decline 139
    Whispers from the Universe 140
    Providing After Death. .140
Potty-Training. 141
Gas. 143
Graffiti. 143
Stupid Ads (YouTube) 144
The (Power) Struggle is Real. 144
Ghosts. 145

Present Moment Mindfulness 146
Cheerleading and 6-packs 148
Adulting 149
Teaching Me 150
Generational Gap—Definition of Sexy 152
To Moustache or Not to Moustache 153
Money 153
 Squeegee Kids 154
 Paying for Chores 154
 Stuff 155
 Financial Know How 156
An Average Day in the Life of a Parent 157
It's Okay to Not Be Okay 160

Summary 161
One Foot Forward 162
If I Could Do It Again … 163
Reaching Perfection 163
Final Words 164

About the Author 165

Introduction

*W*hat is a "perfect" parent? Do they have a perspicacious view of parenting? Do you know anyone you consider to be a "perfect" parent? Or do all parents have inherent flaws? It is my theory there is no such thing as a "perfect" parent.

In this section we explore various definitions of a "perfect" parent. With examples of what our parents did and what we have experienced as parents, we will try to determine what constitutes a "perfect" parent.

In general, people approach things in their own way. Sometimes, as parents, we strive to do things differently than our parents chose to. (I know my experience with liver made me swear to never force my kids to eat something they did not like.) Other times we adopt the skills as they were demonstrated by our parents; perhaps by enforcing rules we were given as children. Our parenting may evolve as we embrace new parenting ideas from formal or informal training. And as we have more children, our perspective and rules may change.

This book is for anyone who is a parent or guardian; those who have been parents will likely relate to and enjoy the book. I write this book from the perspective of a mother, but the advice relates to all genders.

I'm going to share with you stories from my own parenting experience. Some are going to be things I am not proud of; things I have done "wrong" (for lack of a better word). Some are going to be things I am very satisfied I did; things I have done "right." First, though, I think it is important to explore a couple of ideas in order to set the stage.

The Journey

Many people strive to be the "perfect" parent. Some people read up on all the new-fangled child-rearing practices. Some wing it. Some listen to (or even ask for) advice from other people. Let's be honest. When it comes to parenting, it's a journey not a destination. And it's a journey without a roadmap. We make it up as we go along.

We may have an itinerary in the back of our minds when we have a baby. This map may be plotted before the parents-to-be are even pregnant—for example, we will have a specific number of children spaced over a certain period of time; we will have this many boys and that many girls—but this is more of a pencil sketch than a formal map. Life has a way of challenging us at times no matter how well we have planned.

First lesson of parenting: adapt. You are going to have things thrown at you (figuratively *and* literally) at various times in your life that you simply need to deal with. You may approach it differently than the person next to you. No matter what, you need to adjust to life's circumstances. The better you are at taking things in stride, the better you will be as a parent.

This book is *not* a "how-to" manual for parents. It's a collection of *my* experiences as a parent and how I came to the realization that parenting is about your experiences and your journey, not your destination. No one is perfect, no one should *expect* to be perfect, and no one should expect *you* to be perfect. (You mean *I'm* not perfect? Whaaaa?! That's it, I'm fired!)

The Destination

Let's pretend for a moment there is a place called Perfection that is your target destination as a parent. This location is where a group of all the perfect parents are gathered together in a community, celebrating their success.

Imagine a road leading to this destination (our Path). If you were driving down a highway on your way to Perfection, there would, ideally, be one clearly marked exit whereupon if you took that exit, you would end up in the desired location with all the other perfect parents.

My hypothesis as I start this book is that if you do manage to make it to Perfection, you will find the destination empty. No one has made it there. Everyone has been waylaid along the way.

But how? Well, the Path to Perfection is one fraught with detours and setbacks. Most parents completely stray from the Path in order to avoid various obstacles. People tend to set high expectations for themselves when it comes to parenting. They may even get upset and blame themselves for everything they feel they have done "wrong" as a parent. My experience raising children has proven this. I never have proclaimed to be a perfect parent; I acknowledge the fact I am not.

Non-Perfectness

There seems to be a recent trend of recognizing parents are not perfect. A quick Google search will come up with several examples, usually humorous, around the concept of the non-perfect parent. I personally enjoy Home with Casey Huff (https://www.facebook.com/etchedinhome/); Finding Joy—Rachel Martin (http://findingjoy.net/); and Kristina Kuzmic (https://www.facebook.com/KristinaKuzmic/ or http://kristinakuzmic.com/). These ladies (and fellow authors) continue to bring a smile to my face (or a tear to my eye) as I can relate to their posts.

There was a Facebook image with a quote—*To the mum*—it brought me to tears. I was that mom. I *am* that mom.

> *To the mum hiding in her bathroom, needing peace for just one minute, as the tears roll down her cheeks …*
>
> *To the mum who is so tired she feel likes she can't function anymore and would do anything to lay down and get the rest she needs…*
>
> *To the mum sitting in her car, alone, stuffing food in her face because she doesn't want anyone else to see or know she eats that stuff …*

Introduction

To the mum crying on the couch after she yelled at her kids for something little and is now feeling guilty and like she is unworthy ...

To the mum that is trying desperately to put those old jeans on because all she really wants is to look in the mirror and feel good about herself ...

To the mum that doesn't want to leave the house because life is just too much to handle right now ...

To the mum that is calling out for pizza again because dinner just didn't happen the way she wanted it to ...

To the mum that feels alone, whether in a room by herself or standing in a crowd...

You are enough.

You are important.

You are worthy.

This is a phase of life for us. This is a really, really hard, challenging, crazy phase of life.

In the end it will all be worth it. But for now it's hard. And it's hard for so many of us in many different ways. We don't always talk about it, but it's hard and it's not just you.

You are enough.

You are doing your best.

Those little eyes that look up at you—they think you are perfect. They think you are more than enough.

Those little hands that reach out to hold you—they think you are the strongest. They think you can conquer the world.

Those little mouths eating the food you gave them—they think that you are the best because their bellies are full.

Those little hearts that reach out to touch yours—they don't want anything more. They just want you.

Because you are enough. You are more than enough, mama.

You. Are. Amazing. ♥ ♥

Credit: *Latched and Attached* http://latchedandattached.com/ Reprinted with permission.

This post is a good reminder that even though we expect ourselves to be perfect, we aren't. And that's okay. We don't need to feel guilty or inadequate. We are enough.

Our Parents

Many of us, including myself, swore at some point in our lives we would never repeat what, we considered to be, our parents' mistakes. These "mistakes," however, *will* inadvertently influence how you parent. The best you can hope for is to learn from these life experiences.

If your parents were divorced and you saw them fighting constantly in front of you, like mine did, you may learn what not to do because of how it negatively affected you. In my case, I learned how to improve my communication in order to better mitigate arguments. Others may have learned this was the norm and not know any better.

If your parents hit or beat you when you did something wrong, you may choose to not physically discipline your children. Conversely, you might learn, erroneously, that this is how people show love and adopt similar behavior.

Introduction

The nurturing (or lack of it) supplied by your parents will impact how you approach things in life (think nature versus nurture). Regardless, we can still learn from them and make ourselves, as parents, better if we should so choose.

Amazingly We Survived!

My late hubby commented about new rules my middle son's school created for "safety" reasons. The rules themselves are not important; rather, the premise behind them is. Our children, today, live in a safety bubble we did not have as when we were their age. Sometimes, I think we take this a bit too far (more about this shortly).

When you think about it, it's really quite amazing any of the past generations survived at all. Here are some of the things we used to do as examples:

- ∞ Riding in the back of a truck. This was a treat when someone had a three-seater truck with more than three people needing transport. We never worried about "what if" something happened. Rather, we giggled as we were bounced around the truck bed. We survived.

- ∞ Not wearing our seatbelts. If the car even had seatbelts, we often did not wear them. I recall asking a step parent what would happen if there was an accident. His answer was to reach his arm across me and hold me to the seat. It never occurred to me that this would never work in reality, so I accepted this answer. We survived.

- ∞ Sticking our tongue to metal in the winter. No one explained *why* we shouldn't do this. We were only told not to. So, naturally, we tried it. Thankfully, I only stuck the very tip of my tongue to the metal monkey bars so ripping my wet tongue off the frozen metal was not as painful as it could have been if I had actually stuck my whole tongue on the bar like licking an ice cream cone. We survived.

∞ Large tractor tires as play equipment was a favourite at one of my elementary schools. Jumping tire to tire was fun and challenging. Especially jumping from the three enormous tires stacked with two on the bottom as a base and one on top forming a mini pyramid onto the next tire which was planted in the ground sideways; only those who were really brave took this risk while all those who were not stood by and watched with envy. We could have broken bones, but I don't think anyone ever did. We survived.

∞ Remember metal merry-go-rounds where one child would run and push several other children as fast as they could and then the pusher would jump onto the moving merry-go-round? The participants hung on for dear life as the metal death trap whirled around and around. Even when we fell off, we still had fun. And we always tried again. Faster! Faster!

∞ We left cooked food on the cupboard and thawed meat on the counter; long enough to let a plethora of bacteria thrive. We just cooked it up and ate it. No one got sick. Maybe our stomachs were made of cast iron, who knows?

∞ We ate eggs out of the coop, drank unpasteurized milk from the cows, butchered chickens on a stump outside with a dirty ax. Food safety never crossed anyone's mind. Now-a-days though, if you have a bed and breakfast, you can't serve your guests fresh eggs without having them inspected. And dairy farmers can't give away milk unless it's pasteurized (a process that kills not only the bad bacteria but the healthy bacteria as well).

Introduction

- ∞ Swimming unattended. I swam in the small stream behind our mobile home on the reservation without any adults or other children nearby. In the water, I could travel as far as I liked—over dams and around bends. No one owned a life jacket, water wings, or any other type of floatation device. You learned to tread water when it was over your head (without lessons). Common sense dictated the water rules and we did not drown.

- ∞ We played with matches and started fires—both in the wood stove and in pits in the yard. We were careful to keep them contained (though not in an approved fire pit) and put them out afterwards (only *you* can prevent forest fires). We still had fire safety rules but not to the extremes of today. We also burned things we shouldn't have. I remember an aerosol can got into our small garbage pile that we burned from time to time. It made a huge popping noise and shot up 20 feet into the air. And I thought, "Cool! Let's do it again!"

- ∞ I learned to shoot a .22 when I was 11. Our guns were not registered or stored in a secure location and the bullets sat in a box beside the guns. You didn't have to hold a firearm permit either or take a firearm safety course. The rules were implied and quite simple: point the gun where you wanted to shoot (target or animal) and to the ground when not in use. I never treated it as a toy. I never pointed it at anyone and I never killed an animal with it (even though I tried a couple times). I never touched the gun unless an adult was with me. Common sense was *not* dead.

Today it seems we have rules for the sake of rules. That's not always ideal in my opinion. Someone somewhere complained about something and someone else made a rule to stop that something. For example, parade float members used to throw candy into the crowds as they were passing. I remember doing this in Martensville when I was on my dad's pizza shop float. Then we were told we couldn't anymore because someone complained. I don't even think there was ever an incident; I think someone objected a child *could* get hurt and the rest, as they say, is history. No more candy thrown from floats.

We successfully navigated all kinds of hazards when we were young—riding in the back of trucks, lack of seatbelts, sticking our tongues to metal, jumping tractor tires, food un-safety, swimming, matches, and guns. It's truly amazing anyone survived the past generations. Heaven forbid if we should get taken out by a rogue piece of candy thrown from a float.

Wandering for Hours on End

When I was younger, we lived on a reservation in northern Saskatchewan. I remember wandering for hours on end—leaving early in the morning and returning when the sun went down. We never had cell phones, so my mom and step-dad never knew where we were at any given point in time. Sometimes I would go alone and sometimes I would gather a group of kids together.

Mischief was never our plan; we were just curious. We wandered in the bushes, exploring. Sometimes we found animals to watch. The occasional wild strawberry got eaten; another tasty treat involved cracking fresh hazelnuts with my teeth after picking them off the bush and peeling off the prickly outer cover. The puffy mushroom-type plants that exploded when you stepped on them were always a fun surprise; I liked how the powder poofed out into the air and settled on the ground.

We rarely entered populated areas, keeping strictly to wooded ones. Whether that was smart or not is to be debated.

Sure, no one could ever find us to kidnap us, but no one could ever *find* us either.

Activities included swimming in Little Red River (no rules about an adult staying within arm's length); general exploring; being at one with nature (okay, that was never our goal, but it sounds good). I don't remember what all we did but we were never bored.

Fast forward to today. I live in a little bit of a rougher neighbourhood—"The Hood Light" I call it. My neighbours don't speak to me (or anyone else). We keep to ourselves. When there were younger children on the block (the same age as my middle child, D), I really struggled to even permit D to go three doors down to visit these kids. Some of it was paranoia something would happen to him, but I think mostly it's because I'm scared of the neighbourhood. And I don't know my neighbours. On the odd occasion, I will take time to go over and introduce myself. Because many of the units are rental units, the turnover is quite high so just when D starts to get to know someone, they move.

Yes, I'm bordering on becoming one of those over-protective parents but more so because society has changed.

Normal Dysfunctional

What is your definition of "normal?" I don't even think the best psychologists in the world can give a clear, universal definition of normal. If the definition is how the majority of people act, what's to say they are right? If the majority of people steal from others, does that mean they are "normal?"

What is normal when it comes to a family? Your mom and dad being married? Two parent families? Blood relatives only? What about adoptive or foster parents? What about step-siblings? Gay/lesbian marriages? Non-conventional marriages? Common-law couples? Single parents? Grandparents raising grandkids? Is any "family" structure "normal?" And, if so, by whose definition?

In my family, my mom and dad divorced when I was five. My brother lived with my dad and I lived with my mom. Both parents re-married (several times) and my dad had children with other women. I don't even know my half-brothers and sisters (before and after me). Hell, I didn't even meet some of my dad's wives. Is this "normal?"

I had a child out of wedlock. I married young. The man I married was, for all intents and purposes, my oldest child's dad—whether by blood or not. I had another child with the man I first married. We then got divorced. Then I re-married and my late husband helped me raise both my children. Is this "normal?"

I don't think any family or family relationship is "normal"—I like to say we are all "normal dysfunctional." We all have our issues and we will all raise our children differently. At the end of the day, who cares if what you are doing is normal? If it works for you and it works for your kid(s), then who is anyone to judge you?

The next time someone says something about being abnormal or dysfunctional, remember, it is *normal* to be this way. Simply smile and state, "I put the fun in dysfunctional."

Passing Judgment

How many of you admit to judging other parents? Honestly. You see a child throwing a tantrum in a supermarket and think, "if I was the parent, I would…" Really? Put yourself in that other parent's shoes for a minute. Maybe they had a bad day at work. Maybe they have personal issues going on. Perhaps they just don't know how to deal with their child's temper tantrum.

As a former "judger," I have to mentally re-align my thoughts when I start to tell myself a story about another person's parenting skills. Instead of judging, offer a hand. I'm sure it will be much more appreciated by that person (who is probably embarrassed by their child's behavior at that moment) than your judgment.

Sometimes it's as simple as an acknowledgement that you empathize. Crack a joke to make them smile. Offer to help; maybe distract the child or have your child engage the other child. This will make an enormous difference to that parent (and that child).

Don't judge other parents. It's wrong; and yes, I meant to use this word.

There Are Children in Other Countries ...

How many Canadian children have heard this nonsense? Eat everything on your plate because, "there are children in other countries who have no food to eat." Yes, it is a tragedy that there are, indeed, children in other countries who have little or no food to eat. (This topic could fill another book by itself.) That begs the question: is me eating everything on my plate going to ensure those in other countries will have more food to eat? No.

As a child, I was often forced to eat what was on my plate. I believe this is part of the reason I now have an eating disorder and am considered morbidly obese. Not just obese. Morbidly obese.

I remember when my step-mom would make something absolutely disgusting for supper—let's pick on liver, the bane of my existence. She would sit me at the table with this meal in front of me. No matter how much ketchup I piled on top of it, I could not kill the taste of the liver. It was chewy and absolutely horrendous—both in texture and in taste. Forty-five minutes at the dinner table to choke down liver drowned in ketchup (think more ketchup than liver). Honestly, pack it up and send it to these starving kids; I doubt they would eat it either.

I swore once I moved out of my parents' home, I would never eat liver again. It's now been 25+ years, and guess what? That's one promise to myself I *have* kept. Besides the odd time I have purchased cat treats with liver in them, that food has not crossed my threshold since I left home.

The rules with my kids are:

- ∞ Try one bite. (Or a few more bites if I feel they haven't eaten enough.)

- ∞ If you don't like it, put it on the side of your plate. (Yes, this means you have to pick *all* the chick peas out of the chili and eat the rest.)

- ∞ No, I won't make you something else. Eat what I've made or don't eat. (No, you won't starve.)

- ∞ *No liver!*

And I never threaten them with the "there are children in other countries …" nonsense. All three of my children are healthy. They are not overweight, and they do not have eating disorders.

Forcing kids to eat more than they want to eat or to eat when they don't want to eat is a bad idea. Even if there are children who are starving in other countries. Is it any wonder why so many kids have eating disorders now-a-days? Granted, it's not the only reason but it definitely contributes to the problem.

Parents Cry

Parents cry. Parents cry because babies cry (see next chapter). Seriously though, parents cry, and this is normal. If you find yourself with a case of the "baby blues" for more than a couple weeks after the baby is born (and this goes for moms *and* dads), you may be suffering from postpartum depression.

I highly recommend a visit to your family doctor. Anti-depressants aren't evil. I've been on them for nine years now and I think they are a god send. Post-partum symptoms started after I had my first child, B, but I did not know at the time what I do now. At one point in my life, I recognized the symptoms of depression because my mom had been diagnosed, so I tried Effexor but found it "zombified" me. I didn't react to anything. When I had my second child, D, I recognized the post-partum symptoms right away. I knew I needed to try anti-depressants again. Thankfully, my doctor prescribed Sertraline, which stabilized my moods and yet still let me feel things appropriately. The mood fluxes are not as severe as they used to be.

Read up on the topic. "The Smiling Mask" was a book I read after I had my second child. A lady I had worked with co-authored it. I realized in reading one of the lady's stories that I did, indeed, have post-partum depression. It was a mild version, but it was still depression. That was the moment when I recognized I had it with my older child as well; I simply never had it diagnosed.

It may take a couple of tries to find the anti-depressant and dose that works for you, but it's worth exploring if you are having issues. And yes, dads, guys get it too—don't be too macho to get it checked out.

Babies Cry

My co-worker, L, called me from China one day (he was on parental leave for his first child) and said to me, "Dawn, I'm a bad dad."

"L," I said, "what makes you say that?"

"My baby cries all the time," he replied.

I started laughing. I couldn't help it. "L," I said, "that's what babies do. They eat, sleep, poop, and cry."

Advising him not to worry, I proceeded to give him some advice on what I did to help calm my children when they were little:

- Car rides—although booting around the city at 4 a.m. is a little extreme, most children find the movement of the car soothing and go right to sleep. Until you stop. (And my last child, T, doesn't like the car at all so that didn't work with him.)
- Hold your baby—use a snuggly or sling or whatever else to keep baby close to you. They were in the womb for nine months; they are used to hearing mom's heartbeat and her voice. It was warm and snuggly inside mom and they crave that feeling.
- Co-sleep (more on this in future chapters)—some babies just don't like being alone.
- Swings—I had a manual crank Graco swing that worked with all my kids. Now you can get ones that require batteries, but I found the old-school one worked best.
- Bouncy chairs—some babies like them and some don't.
- Jolly jumpers—the best invention *ever*. You can get ones that hook to doorways or ones that stand alone. I still have a video of D going to town (having a lot of fun) in his.
- Exersaucers—there are a plethora of these available with different options: toys, music, colours, etc.

Babies cry. That's life. Remember when I said that as parents, we must adapt? Case in point.

Introduction

Right and Wrong

As it stands, I don't consider myself a perfect parent. However, I also struggle with saying I've done things "wrong" or "right" as a parent. According to the dictionary (www.m-w.com), the definition of "right" is *being in accordance with what is just, good, or proper*. Being "wrong" implies exactly the opposite. It infers you were mistaken or incorrect in your parenting behavior. It may even suggest you have injured or inflicted harm to your children based on your parenting skills. Naming the following book sections was hard for me. The first draft for Part 1 was "Things That I have Done Wrong." But were they wrong? They worked for me at the time, given the skills and tools I had.

My three children range in age from three to 23. That's a substantial age difference. I was young when I had my first child. Considering there was no parenting guide back then and people didn't blog about their failures as a parent, we made it through. She turned out okay. (More than okay but I don't want to brag.)

I truly believe (most) parents do the best they can with what they have. I don't think people set out to do things "wrong" as a parent. Most strive to treat their children well and bring their kids up to the best of their ability. When I refer to parents, I am talking about these people—not the anomalies out there who intentionally hurt kids.

The following stories are true tales from my parenthood path. They were written over an eight-year span between 2010 and 2018 so you may find some inconsistencies in the timeline or variations in writing style. Regardless, I hope you enjoy them.

PART 1

Things That Could Have Been Done Differently

As I stated in the introduction, parenting is like a journey without a road map. There is no "how-to" guide for new parents with step-by-step instructions. On-the-job experience is the only way we learn to be parents. We know the theory: raise these itty-bitty humans into fully functional, responsible adults with morals and empathy. And we provide the basics: food, water, and shelter. We all love our children, but we are learning as we go. This section is filled with examples of lessons others might consider "wrong" or that I might do differently now. Examples such as using TV as a babysitter, swearing, and discipline. Buckle up, this part of the road is rough; it's subject to bumps, potholes, and last-minute swerving around obstacles.

Let Her Cry

B, my first child, came into my life when I was 19. Since I had no experience with younger children, I often sought out the advice of other people. "Let her cry," was the advice I got from my mother. This seemed to be her solution for everything. Even when transitioning B off her bedtime bottle.

And so, I did. For 45 gut-wrenching minutes. It (sadly) worked but looking back, it was not the way I should have done things. And it's not the way I did things with my next two children.

I have never understood why people decide to let their children cry for extended periods of time. Not only is it hard for the child, it is heart-breaking for the parent (at least it was for me). The child is trying to communicate something to you and yet you, as the parent, let them cry and ignore them. Now, I'm not talking about the whiny, attention-seeking cry or the fake crying; I'm referring to the all out the-world-is-ending cry. The one that results in the child (possibly) throwing up or the one where the child is physically hurt.

I have since decided that no matter what, my child will not be left to cry for extended periods of time. I realize children will cry and you may not be able to stop them from crying; however, it is important to pick them up to reassure them you are there, and they are safe. I don't consider it spoiling the child or coddling; I consider it good parenting.

Tylenol

As previously mentioned, I was a young mom. I didn't know a lot about babies. B's biological dad had a child before. So, when he suggested we give our newborn baby Tylenol to sleep, I thought nothing of it.

He gave our child 1 ml of baby Tylenol. She slept alright. For over 12 hours! I took her to the doctor at hour number eight. Not realizing we had done anything wrong, I admitted we had given her baby Tylenol. My doctor, not at all astonished, calmly informed me newborns did not need that much baby Tylenol and it wasn't to be used to help her sleep.

Lesson learned. Find another way to get baby to sleep.

Co-Sleeping

Back in 1995 when I had my first child, it was almost unheard of to have a teen parent. My "education" about child-rearing consisted of a few tidbits from various people and books I read. And so, for my first child, I struggled through breastfeeding and trying (not always successfully) to have B sleep in the crib. I cried. I drove around the city at 4 a.m. I cried more. Finally, on those really trying nights, I dozed off beside B while she was nursing. Those were some of the best nights' sleeps I got. Yet I never quite clued into the notion of co-sleeping. (I don't even think the term was coined at this time.) I still tried to get my baby to sleep in her crib.

Then we moved into a twin bed. And my toddler wanted me to lie with her, which I, grudgingly, did. For 10 to 30 minutes at a time. All the while thinking about what else I could be doing—usually studying, as I was in first year university at the time.

I had my second child, D, in 2009. By then I had a lot more knowledge and many of my friends had children by then. I heard about co-sleeping and did a bit of research on it. Thank goodness for Google. I decided this was something worth pursuing, especially since my ex-husband worked nights. As my ex had insomnia, I not want D to wake my ex up by crying. Add to that the fact I was pretty much taking care of the baby by myself at nights (my ex worked graveyard shifts). Co-sleeping allowed me to keep my sanity and get the rest I needed.

D and I migrated to the spare room where we happily co-slept for almost 2 years. When I had to nurse, I simply had to whip out a breast, pull baby to it, and doze back off to sleep. I nursed D until he was about nine months, but we continued to co-sleep because it worked. And all was good and happy in the world. After that, it was just nice to have him sleep by me.

With my third child, T, born in 2015, my late spouse, J, indicated he did not want to co-sleep with baby. I tried not to. We kept a bassinet by the bed. T was waking up every couple of hours (as babies do). I tried to put him back in the bassinet after every nursing but sometimes I fell asleep before he was done feeding. Within a few weeks, J caved. Baby was now co-sleeping with us. It's been two and a half years (at the time of writing).

This brings me to another topic about co-sleeping. How do small children take up so much room? We had a queen size bed when we had T. Within a couple weeks, we upgraded to a king size. After J passed, it was just T and I in that massive bed and I *still* managed to be segregated to one quarter of the bed while my 30-pound toddler sprawled out across the remaining three quarters of the (king size) bed. By the morning, he was snuggled right up against me—which should have been a nice feeling—but, as I was falling out of bed, I couldn't really enjoy it.

Now I think I procrastinate moving T into his own bed because the king size bed would be lonely to sleep in on my own. Soon though, I promise, I will make a more concerted effort. Soon.

Hurry Up!

"We're late. We're late. For a very important date. No time to say hello, good-bye. We're late. We're late. We're late." (Alice in Wonderland)

After having D (fourteen years after my first child) I forgot no matter how far ahead you start getting ready, you can never seem to get out the door and where you need to be (on time). My friends started realizing when I said I'd be there at 2 p.m., I really meant 2:30 p.m. Or even later. I was becoming one of those people who was perpetually late for everything.

Thankfully, as your child gets older this gap gets smaller and you start to get places on time. However, some days getting your five-year-old to put on his sweater, jacket, and boots is like pulling teeth. (Only more painful.)

One of my co-workers was telling me she took her child into work with her one day and introduced her child to her boss. She told her child that her boss yells at her every time she is late (and her boss backed her up). Though it wasn't exactly true (yes, we all lie to our children at some point) it proved a point that there were repercussions when we are late to things. Her child cooperated getting ready after that.

I haven't tried that yet with T, but I think it's a brilliant way to show natural consequences.

Now, take the times when we are going somewhere fun, like It's a Blast or Dino Bouncers. Do you think I need to nag my boy to get ready those times? No ... he has to nag me. "Come on Mom, let's go!" He can have his stuff on quicker than the blink of an eye on those days.

Kids can hurry when they want to (when they want something) but when *you* want them to hurry, good luck getting them to move at anything faster than a snail's pace.

Television IS a Great Babysitter

Back when I was in university (1996—2002), I needed more sleep than my young daughter would let me have. So, when I had a late night and wanted to sleep in I would use TV as a babysitter.

We had a hide-a-bed; an old-school, ugly, floral, heavy-ass hide-a-bed. On the mornings I wanted to sleep in, B would wake me up, we would drag ourselves downstairs to the living room, I would open the hide-a-bed, and pop a Disney VHS into the VCR. (Wow, talk about dating myself.) B would enjoy the video while I got some much-needed rest.

There was a golden rule, though. If B had to leave the hide-a-bed for *any* reason, she would wake me up. If she left the bed without telling me, the movie was done. Funny thing, I never had a problem. She always stayed right beside me.

Yes, I know, parents aren't supposed to use TV as a babysitter, but I don't think I ever would have kept my sanity if it wasn't for a good stock of Disney VHS's and a VCR. And I definitely wouldn't have finished university.

Electronics ARE Great Babysitters

Fast forward 20 years. My daughter, who is now 23, made a comment to me one night when we were out for supper after I had handed her younger brothers my cell phone to watch something on YouTube, "Mom, you shouldn't always use the cell phone to distract the boys."

I smiled as I replied, "It's so I can eat in peace." I, personally, would rather have my boys, especially the youngest, watching YouTube quietly at the table instead of running around, yelling, and disturbing the other guests. Oh, who's kidding who? It's so he won't disturb *me*.

Ideal? No. I spent many months after that remembering what she said as I relinquished my cell phone to distract the boys. Yes, I rely on electronics to distract my children, especially the youngest one. He can now navigate YouTube like a pro. He switches videos whenever he wants to. And I get time to do those (important) things like cleaning the house, playing my own games, and writing my book.

Ironically, yesterday when we went over to my daughter's new house, I noticed when she needed to distract T, she whipped out her cell phone and put on YouTube. I chuckled to myself and said nothing.

Boxes Rule!

One birthday I bought my son, D, a $100 Lego set. For those of you who don't know, $100 worth of new Lego does not go very far any more. You get several small pieces and dozens of little circular (useless) single dot Legos. Very few 2 X 4 bricks are in the box now-a-days. You are better off buying used Lego. But I digress.

Like most toys, they get played with for a while then they get shoved into a corner and forgotten about.

My late husband bought a Bow-Flex. It came in a HUGE box. One that was taller than D. With a roll of packing tape, a pair of scissors, markers, and some imagination, we made a play house. It had a door, two windows, a fire alarm and decorations (in marker). It took up most of the living room and we had to keep moving it out of the way, but this "toy" kept D's attention much longer than any store-bought toy every did.

I think we've resolved to not buy any more $100 toys. Instead, gather large boxes from wherever you can and make a small fort or city out of them. Decorate and rebuild as necessary. Discard and replace when they get ratty.

Note, any household pets may try to claim the play house as their own. Our cats all loved the cardboard boxes.

Boxes are the best toys *ever*! For parents, kids and pets alike.

Why You Should Not Let Your Kids Believe in Santa Claus

"Here comes Santa Claus, here comes Santa Claus, right down Santa Claus Lane. He's got a bag that's filled with toys for boys and girls the same. Hear those sleigh bells jingle jangle, all is merry and bright. So, jump in bed and cover up your head 'cause Santa Claus comes tonight." (A popular Christmas carol.)

Ah, the joys of Christmas. Along with Christmas comes the joy of Santa Claus; all the young children are on their best behavior for fear Santa will leave them lumps of coal instead of a gift. The following is a modified speech I wrote for Toastmasters on why you should not let your kids believe in Santa Claus.

For hundreds of years, children have believed in Santa Claus, a fat, jolly, bearded old man dressed in a red suit lined with white fur. A figure whose roots can be traced back to a real person—Saint Nicholas. In many countries across the world, including Canada, children are taught if they are good, then this fat jolly old man will slide down chimneys leaving gifts for all the good little boys and girls. The bad boys and girls will be left a lump of coal.

Like most young children, I gullibly accepted that this fat, jolly, bearded old man was real. The fresh milk and cookies I eagerly left out every Christmas Eve had disappeared by the time I awoke each Christmas Day. One year I even left him a pail of water for his thirsty reindeer.

I was never one of those intelligent kids who analyzed things about Santa Claus and determined early on that he was not real. Oh no! I fully believed.

I never contemplated how Santa Claus could travel all around the world to get to all the houses in just one night. (Which, I now know, would have to be several times faster than the speed of light.)

I never questioned how this fat, jolly, bearded old man could get into *every* house regardless of whether they had a chimney or not. In fact, the one year when I asked this, I was told he could get in through *any* opening.

It never bothered me that this old reclusive man could get into everyone's houses *sans* key. In fact, you never quite knew what time of the night he got there, just that he would.

I never clued into the fact all the presents from Santa Claus were wrapped in the same wrapping as those my mother wrapped or that Santa Claus' writing looking surprisingly similar to hers.

It never dawned on me Santa Claus couldn't really be in several malls in the same city at the exact same time. I was just happy to be able to go and visit him in whatever mall we happened to be at.

I never realized the fact that no matter what I asked Santa Claus for, I never got it. I was always too thrilled to have new toys to play with each Christmas.

I was *completely* oblivious to the fact that Santa Claus was not real; my parents had me completely snowed.

Like so many kids, I believed whole heartedly in this (generous) fat, jolly, bearded old man who left me gifts like clockwork every Christmas. Every year, I would beg my mom to take me to go see him. I would go and sit on his lap, give him my wish list and have my picture taken with him (back before malls charged exorbitant amounts for these pictures). I'd even write him letters some years. Every year until Grade 6 that is.

After a particularly long day in the city, one which my mom had *promised* me that I could go see Santa Claus, I was nagging her to stop by the mall. And I have to admit I was quite adamant about it. I begged and pleaded. My mom's husband at the time, had apparently had enough and crushed my beliefs with these five words: "Santa Claus is not real."

<STOP>

WHAT?!? What do you mean Santa Claus is not real? I looked to my mother with pleading in my eyes. Surely, I had heard wrong. She would correct him! Alas, this was not the case. I was shattered! I simply could not believe it. Santa Claus not real?

And so ended this childhood fantasy. To this day, I do not see how adults could be so cruel. Feeding their children lies about a fat, jolly, old man who brings presents to all the good little boys and girls. Threatening them with "you'll get a lump of coal in your stocking."

It was the most heart-wrenching experience of my young fragile life to find out Santa Claus was not real. It scarred me for life.

The point of my story today was to tell you why *you* should not let *your* kids believe in Santa Claus. If they don't figure it out using common sense, you will traumatize your child when you tell him or her at a later date—like my mom's secomd husband did to me. Save them the grief. Do not lie to them and do not let them believe in that fat, jolly, bearded old man whose belly shakes when he laughs like a bowl full of jelly.

Call My New Spouse "Mom" or "Dad"

My daughter's biological dad insisted B call his new girlfriend "Mom." It bothered me, a lot, though I don't exactly know why. Maybe because I was so young, and I thought "Mom" was me and no one else could do it. I also didn't like the fact he got mad at her if she didn't. She was young and wanted to make us both happy.

After my first marriage ended, I did not ask my daughter or my son to call my late spouse "Dad." My daughter was older and just called him by his first name. My son called him "My J." D used to correct people when they called J his Dad but not so much anymore. While he doesn't call J "Dad," he accepts if someone else assumes it.

It comes down to what your child is comfortable with. Maybe someday, "My J" will become "Dad."

Germs

I have never considered myself to be a germaphobe. A healthy amount of germs keeps the body healthy. To a point. That being said …

My mom was in the hospital and we had gone down to the Robin's Donuts (which resided in the hospital). My son was four. We were in line to make a purchase. I had asked him which donut he wanted. He chose one and remained by the donut display. I, meanwhile, moved to the cashier to place our order. I turned towards him to confirm his donut choice and watched, in horror, as my son ran his tongue up the length of the donut display case.

I yelled in disgust, "D! Do not lick the display case!" I was horrified, mortified, and worried about all the disgusting germs this display case had on it. Not only was it a display case, it was in a hospital—one with sick people in it.

Other people in the line chuckled. Well, they actually laughed out loud.

Looking back, I can see the humour in it. My son didn't die; he didn't even get sick. I guess the experience proves the point that germs are not necessarily a bad thing. But I still wouldn't recommend licking the display case where the donuts are. Especially in a hospital.

***

One day we were out grocery shopping. We got to the front to pay. I was moving groceries from my cart to pay for them when I glanced over and caught D licking the conveyor belt. Seriously? Yes, seriously.

"What are you doing?" I inquired.

He smiled and replied, "Nothing."

I just shook my head.

***

And then there was my youngest child. I caught him licking the floors at Walmart. Ew, ew, ew!

***

Given all the germs my boys have ingested, it's no wonder they hardly get sick. And when they do get sick, they get over it quickly. That's a positive, I guess.

Personally, I'd rather have them build their immunity by taking in germs then treating everything with sanitizer, thus creating super bugs. Don't even get me started on the overuse of antibiotics in our society.

Still, I don't recommend licking the donut case, the conveyer belt, or the floor at a store. Not on purpose anyway.

Bubble Wrap

I wish we could bubble wrap our kids, so they didn't get hurt. I never hit my kids; but when they got bumps and bruises, I felt all the worse, like people were judging me for failing as a parent.

Case in point: T came barreling into the bathroom the other day and slammed his face into the tub resulting in a black eye. Yeah, that looks really good on a (then) thirteen-month-old. Not!

When she was two, my daughter somehow managed to walk into the flush handle on our toilet, resulting in a black eye. I'm still not sure how as there was little to no room between the toilet and the sink. Just talented, I guess.

Then there was the time I got a call at work from daycare one day explaining that my (then) three-year-old daughter had walked into the swing on the playground. She had to get butterfly stitches on her eye.

My daughter has had a broken arm twice. Once from falling out of a tree (not in my care at the time) and once from climbing over the six-foot high fence surrounding our back yard. Irony? Regarding the latter, she was a young adult at the time and didn't want to "wake me up" by knocking. Instead, she had to wake me up to take her to the hospital and sit there for 12 hours while we waited for an X-ray. Next time, I relayed to her, just wake me up *before* trying to climb the fence.

Then there was the time she fell off the trampoline and needed to take an ambulance ride from the farm to the city. Granted, she was in her biological father's care at the time not mine, so the blame resided with him.

And the self-imposed injuries are funny sometimes too. Like walking into a pole while texting. Is it any wonder my daughter's nickname in school (from a teacher) was "Band-Aid?"

My youngest son has taken to head butting everything. We're not sure why. But he has a cacophony of bruises on his head at any given point in time.

My middle son, D, was pretending to be a cat and didn't see the wall in front of him. When I asked him what happened he explained, rationally, that the wall jumped out and hit him.

Playing Superman and "flying off the couch." *sigh*

At least D hasn't tried to climb down over the side of his "fort bed" swinging like a monkey. Wait, I spoke too soon.

And what's with walking around with your hands in your pocket? D learned he can't pull his hands out fast enough when he needs to catch himself because he tripped on a completely flat surface. Resulting in a massively bruised and scraped face. (Face plant!)

My ex was once playing tag with B in the townhouse we lived in. They were running around having a blast but he wasn't watching where he was going and ran right into the pole that our clothing line was secured to. He hit it so fast, it knocked him flat on the ground. Of course, I rushed over to see if he was okay but I was laughing while doing it. After he recovered, he laughed too.

Then there's me. At 42, I decided I was going to roller skate. The last time I did that was at the roller derby when I was 15. Unfortunately, it's not like riding a bike—where once you know how to do it, you are good for the rest of your life. I strapped those roller skates on (yes, the ones with four wheels as they were "safer") and stood up. I moved two steps and the roller skates went forward while I went backward. Bam. Broken wrist. That will teach me to try to relive my youth!

Bubble wrap would be a good thing. Especially for the parents.

Just Being Dumb

We bought our first house when my daughter was 12. She had a room downstairs while ours was upstairs. This happened the first week we moved in.

Our new dog, Ginger, started growling in our bedroom late one night. We kept trying to shush her. She finally stopped.

Then our phone rang. It was one o'clock in the morning. My mom was calling to tell me B was locked downstairs in the sump pump room.

We, of course, freaked (at the rude awakening) and ran downstairs. Our first instinct? Not to ask if she was okay. Not to be rational. No, it was to yell at her for 15 minutes asking questions like: Why didn't she just call us? What was she thinking? How long was she in there? How dumb was she to lock herself in there? What the hell?

She decided, for whatever reason, to go into the sump pump room and shut the door behind her—after we went to bed. Effectively locking herself in as unbeknownst to her, there was no door handle on the inside of the sump pump room door. Of course, she denied it at first, trying to tell us the door had just shut on its own—until we showed her it couldn't possibly happen. Oh, and she just happened to have the home phone receiver with her.

So, her solution? Call her friends and talk on the phone for two hours. Wait for her dad to get up for work at 3 a.m. and then knock on the door. When she got bored of that, then call Grandma to call us to come to her rescue.

Eventually, we did calm down and ask if she was okay. The next day, we installed a door handle on the inside of the door.

Throwing Teddy Bears

I remember one day coming back from work. My niece and nephew were living with us at the time. When I got home, I looked at my niece's face. She had a huge gash under her eye. When I asked what happened I was told, despite being told not to throw things in the house, my daughter and niece had been tossing a soft, squishy teddy bear up into the air and catching it. Now, a teddy bear is fairly safe. You would expect no one could get hurt throwing a stuffy around, right? Not so. Somehow, this teddy bear had hit the overhead light shade (one of the old school square ones that hung down and wasn't overly secured). The light shade burst into several pieces and a large shard fell and hit my niece just under the eye.

Lesson learned. Even the very softest toy being mishandled will cause injury.

Swear Words

You've heard that old adage kids are sponges. Well, they are. And they may not indicate they've even heard something you've said until sometime in the future, when you are least expecting it.

I am not great at watching my swearing around the kids. I will apologize to them if I say something inappropriate. I also try not to use certain swear words which I consider worse than others. Yeah, I know, it's not logical. But I try not to use the word "cunt" or "mother-fucker" for example.

Anyway, one day I was driving a friend and her husband around apartment shopping. We stopped at one place in the north end. My daughter was with me; she was around nine or ten at the time. She started laughing as she pointed at one of the names on the buzzer board. I asked what she was laughing at. She pointed at the last name (Kuntz) and said, "That name spells 'cunts'."

I was mortified. Instead of correcting her pronunciation though, I instead inquired (loudly), "Where on earth did you hear that horrid word?"

"You said it in traffic one day," was her reply.

My friends thought this was hilarious and burst out laughing.

I was even more mortified at this, but I quickly dropped the subject.

Lesson learned. Kids are sponges and pick up everything, so watch what you say in front of them.

Candy Shop

"I'll take you to the candy shop. I'll let you lick the lollipops. Keep going girl, just don't stop. Keep going till you hit the spot. Whoo!"

My daughter came home from Grade 4 singing these 50 Cent lyrics—courtesy of the friendly neighbourhood bus driver. I was horrified. Absolutely horrified.

What did I do about it? Ashamedly, I did not broach the topic with the bus driver or even the school board. That's what I think I should have done.

Instead I tried, unsuccessfully, to explain to my young daughter what the lyrics were about. Not an appropriate topic for someone in Grade 4. Fortunately, I realized this and stopped after saying, "It's about sex."

Kids don't always understand what the lyrics of a song are about (thankfully). In hindsight, I probably should have just shrugged it off and not made a big deal of it. Children will be exposed to all kinds of things their parents dread. Being open and honest with your kids is a good policy—to their age limit.

Discipline

My daughter was very young; I don't remember exactly how old. I remember I gave her a spanking. Once. Now, I did not use a wooden spoon like my step mom used on me; I opted for a flat hand—on her bottom—over her clothes rather than on bare skin. I did not hit her hard enough to leave a mark, but I did it firm enough to make an impression on her. She cried; I cried; and then I apologized. A lot. I don't know who felt worse, me or my daughter. All I know is I swore I would never do it again.

When I was growing up, discipline was doled out as a smack with a wooden spoon or a hand. It was nothing to be put over my mom's knee (until I grew big enough that this was impossible). That was before they made it a law not to hit a child. And for the most part I agree with this. Parents should not be able to hit their children.

Imagine if as adults we solved our problems by hitting each other. I'm talking about in our day-to-day life. I know some people do this already. Say someone cuts you off in a line and instead of just saying, "please do not butt in" you wound up and slugged them. Or if you made a mistake in your computer coding at work and your boss hit you instead of explaining what you did wrong and letting you correct it. It would be a vastly different world and not one I would want to live in.

Now I'm not saying we shouldn't use discipline. I'm just saying we should not use physical discipline. There are plenty of other ways to correct behavior, such as grounding or timeouts.

Furthermore, I find imposing physical discipline is not always necessary to correct the behaviour. Sometimes a stern look or a simple statement like "I am disappointed" will often do the trick. Most times children are smart enough to know when they have done something wrong. Like the family dog that hangs its head when it has pooped inside. (Not that your child is a dog.) My point is, your child can (and should) learn their behaviour was not appropriate in ways other than physical discipline.

Holidays after Divorce or Separation

Lots of divorce/separation agreements provide clauses for how holidays will be dispersed—usually alternating between the parents.

In the beginning, after my first separation (from B's biological dad), I got "stuck" on wanting my daughter on holidays. The actual holidays. Over the years, it became less important to celebrate on the actual date and more important that we just held the celebration on any day.

After my divorce from my ex-husband, this became a non-issue. It became more about adjusting around work schedules and ensuring everyone had time to visit around the holiday. Some years, for example, I would get my Christmas holidays the week after or the week before Christmas. It didn't matter to me if it was "my year" for Christmas. If I had holidays, I would ask my ex for those days for Christmas and defaulted the actual days (Dec 25/26) to him. He always had those days off work (as did I) but he often could not get time before or after those dates because he worked for a shipping company (ironically, unloading and shipping parcels and Christmas gifts to other people).

Funnily enough, this helped in other areas of my life as well, like when family was available to participate in the holidays. Sometimes my daughter when she got older would ask to have a holiday on another day. And so, we would.

It makes life so much easier to plan your holiday when *you* want it versus when the calendar dictates.

Rules for the Sake of Rules

My ex liked to make rules for the sake of rules. "Because I said so," was his default response. No explanation; no rhyme or reason. Just a rule. No room for negotiation. "My way or the highway."

I hated that. Maybe it's the rebel inside of me struggling to get out. Who knows? I just know a rule without a reason is silly.

For example, being home at an *exact* time. If my daughter was told to be home at 8 p.m. and she walked in at 8:03 p.m., she was grounded (by my ex). Even if it was because of a delay in traffic. I, personally, did not understand why three minutes mattered. A longer period of time—like 30 minutes—yes, I would be concerned. But three minutes? "She needs to be more responsible," was the reason I got.

Even if she called to say she would be late, my ex still would ground her. It was unacceptable to him that she be even a moment late on a previously dictated rule. It was beyond my comprehension.

One counsellor we saw suggested my ex was a brick wall parent and I was a marshmallow parent. Neither are good parenting styles.

My generation was the one that had males cover up their earrings with bandaids when working at McDonald's. Society, at the time, dictated only females were to have their ears pierced. This was before Human Rights legislation dictated you treat everyone the same; if one gender could wear something to work, so could the other.

In high school, a friend of mine got her eyebrow pierced and her parents made her take it out. She still has a slight scar there.

Based on my experience growing up, I thought piercing belonged only on the ears. I was accepting of both genders having pierced ears (even my brother who had both pierced—most men only pierce one side).

When I reached university, I had the top of my ear pierced; that was the furthest I would go.

At one pub in Saskatoon, you could get your nipple pierced for free as long as you did it on stage in front of everyone. Ouch! That's a pretty sensitive area; not one I would want a needle pushed through just for fun. I remember wondering why people (especially women) would want to get this done. Of course, I was a mom by then and nipples had a more practical use for me as I breastfed all my children.

That was *my* rule for the sake of rules. Mine. Piercings were for ears. Period. End of story.

My daughter wanted to get her belly button pierced when she was a teenager; we did a lot of research and I did a lot of internal soul searching before I agreed to let her have it done. Guess what? She didn't die; and neither did I. She even drew me a picture of both of us with our belly buttons pierced (that motivated me to try to lose weight for a while). I never had the stomach for a belly button piercing (pun fully intended).

Years later, I stepped outside my comfort zone and went with B to have our noses pierced. It didn't hurt as much as I thought it would (except when D would try to pull it out as a baby); I didn't get judged as much as I thought I would either (in fact, I think people treated me better because of it—strange, I know). B still has hers but mine has grown over since. It was a combination of events—having the stud ripped from my nose on multiple occasion by the grasping fingers of my infant son and losing the stud one day causing it to heal over. Who knows, I might get up the nerve to do it again.

By this point in time, piercing was much more commonplace in society—ears, eyebrows, nipples, tongues, chins. Now there are even dermal piercings which I just don't understand but who knows—maybe I'll change my mind in the future.

Despite my not being a social butterfly, my daughter was. She wanted to date boys around age 14 (I think) but our rule (for the sake of rules) was no dating until age 16. Not because we didn't trust our daughter. Just because. It took a lot of discussion to convince my ex otherwise. Her first boyfriend was when she was 15.

Apparently, being a guy, my ex knew what went through boys' minds. Grown men (my ex and my late husband) both seemed to be able to discern what boys were thinking because, "they were boys once." Like they could mind read what every boy was thinking. All the time.

Just like my late ex mother-in-law, Nana, was adamant we were going to have a rough time raising a teenage girl because of *her* experience with her adopted daughter. Nana had the audacity to say to B one time (when she was around 19), "I'm glad you turned out so well. I had my doubts." Or something to that effect. Nana was a master at making a compliment sound like an insult. But I digress. Back to B dating.

After I managed to arm twist my ex hubby into allowing B to date at 15, the next hurdle was allowing her to visit her boyfriend's house. Now I'm not talking about an afternoon of mischief with no adults around. I'm talking one where there was adult supervision—the boy's mother, who was one of my daughter's teachers at the time, was going to be home. Again, a long, drawn out discussion that, in my opinion, didn't need to happen.

Eventually, I had to call the boy's mother and explain what was going on. She had the opinion we didn't trust her and that wasn't it at all. Thankfully we smoothed things over and B and this boy dated for about a year.

Being a single parent is hard. I often use YouTube to distract the boys while I am getting ready for work or they are eating breakfast in the morning. It works for us.

The other day, B was over after work and she mentioned they were lucky because when she was their age, she had to walk 5 miles in the snow, uphill, to get to school. No wait, that wasn't it. She had a rule (for the sake of rules) that she was not allowed any electronics in the morning before school.

Maybe I've become more lenient with experience; or maybe I just need to have a bit of sanity in my life because that rule has been booted from my home.

As I reflect upon this chapter, I realize even *I* made rules that had no rhyme or reason:

- ∞ Your friend can't come over because you asked me five minutes beforehand. Yet, we had nothing going on that a visit would interfere with. I think this was more due to inconvenience.
- ∞ Twenty-four hours' notice for a sleep over. Again, even when we had nothing going on.
- ∞ Cell by the computer at night—for my daughter anyway. The boys like to listen to relaxation music right before sleep. And sometimes I play games on my phone while lying in bed with the boys.
- ∞ Early curfew—by 8 p.m. Okay, in all fairness this one was because my mom's second husband had a (silly) rule that you could not start anything new after 8 p.m. No reason. Just a rule for the sake of rules.

Even I struggle with rules for the sake of rules; sometimes I have to stop and examine why I have set a rule. Many times, I've had to discard a rule if I didn't have a logical reason for it. This comes back to my earlier statement that as parents we must adapt.

You're Wearing What?

One rule (yes, for the sake of rules) I have had to deal with repeatedly over the years with all my children is, "You can't wear that in public." At home, maybe. But in public? Uh uh. *shaking head*

With B, first it was mismatched socks. She would throw all her socks into a container and just grab two at random to wear to school. I was mortified. Socks *had* to match otherwise it looked like we were too poor to clothe our child properly. It really grated on my nerves. Until I realized the brilliance in her decision.

We all know dryers eat socks. It's a scientifically proven fact. (Totally kidding of course.) Though it sure seems like it sometimes. How many of you have a bag or box full of unmatched socks you refuse to throw out because you *might* find the match at some point? I know I do. Even after the kids have grown out of them, I still refuse to toss them in the garbage.

Socks are expensive. And unless you are buying plain white or black socks in bulk, brands differ in colour, size, material, thickness, etc. Even if you buy the same brands, if you choose coloured socks or ones with a pattern, a multi-pack of socks often only contains one pair of the same colour or pattern.

It saves time (folding/matching socks) and money by doing what B was doing—tossing her unmatched socks into a basket and picking two at random. I have embraced this new look; in fact, as I am writing this right now, I am wearing two different colour socks. Now, I do attempt to match socks up in pairs but there are days (usually when I need to do laundry) where I just throw caution to the wind and toss mismatched socks on the boys or myself.

Things That Could Have Been Done Differently

Now holey socks? *That* is a whole different ball of cotton.

Holey pants. Nothing says destitute like pants (jeans, sweats, whatever) with huge rips in the knees (or elsewhere for that matter). Where is your pride child?

And then I saw *why* all the pants got holes in them. And how often. Funny how this only happened with my boys. Boys are rough. Very rough. I can buy D a new pair of pants and he can manage to get holes in the knee on the same day. I watched him one time run down a field and then throw himself on his knees and skid to a stop. Repeatedly. Why? Because the sky was blue, the grass was green, or *shrug*. Seriously?!?

Sears (a large chain department store) had a policy if you bought pants and they got wrecked before your child outgrew them, they would replace them. I would buy them two sizes too big just, so I could save some money. And yes, I used the policy quite often. I wonder if that's part of the reason they went out of business.

I now throw my hands up when D either leaves the house with holey pants or returns home with holes at the knees in his newest set of pants. He just grins and shrugs. So do I.

B has never been what you would call a "girly girl." She rarely wore dresses because of this, even though she thought they were pretty. Plus, dresses weren't really practical when you were as athletic as she was. I think she had a love/hate relationship with them. She owned a few during high school. The prettiness factor won, with one slight modification—she would wear the dress over her jeans.

The Path to Perfection

This fashion choice was before leggings under dresses was popular like it is today (in 2018). She would put a beautiful flowery dress overtop of jeans. At first, I thought it was a poor fashion choice then I started doing it a few years later.

The brilliance of wearing a dress over pants far outweighed my mental protests. I don't like the wind catching my dress and whipping it up over my head. I wore shorts under them for a while and that worked as well. Every time I try to wear nylons, they end up getting snags in them. High heels and I do not see eye to eye. I can (and have) sprained my ankle walking on level ground. No, I'm not kidding. Plus, living in Saskatchewan, the weather can literally be -3 and +16 in the same week; so, wearing pants under a dress makes sense in order to keep warm.

A couple other quick examples of things I *used* to struggle with: wearing pajamas out of the house—some days, that's all I can get T to wear because everything else "hurts." It's not worth the fight to me. Their pajamas cover them better than most summer clothes. And costumes—why not? They cost enough to purchase—the kids might as well get good use out of them. Any time D has worn his Bumblebee or Optimus Prime costume in public, he gets compliments from people. It brings that little bit of joy to him and everyone around him.

When my children choose to wear clothing which I do not approve of (within reason—I say this because I still wouldn't let them go out in just underwear or something crazy like that), instead of questioning, "You're wearing what?" I stop and ask myself the reason(s) for why they might choose to make that new fashion statement. If I can't think of a *real* objection other than I do not approve of it, they can wear it in public. And I don't let it bother me.

Marshmallows versus Brick Walls

During one counselling session early on in our marriage, our counsellor made an observation: I am a marshmallow parent while my ex is a brick wall. Neither one of these is good.

Being a marshmallow implies you are soft (and edible and delicious). LOL! I tended to let my child(ren) persuade me into things. If they had a good, logical reason that made sense, I could be easily swayed. Hell, I still can be. I had rules, but they could be bent a bit (not totally broken, but bent, yes).

Being a brick wall implies you are unmoving. Rules for the sake of rules is your motto. Do as I say, not as I do. And if you cross me, there will be consequences (even if they do not fit the crime). Grounded for one week because you were three minutes late, for example.

Marshmallows and brick walls clash as parental types. Frequently. There is no meshing of parenting styles … even if you try to smoosh the marshmallow all over the brick wall or smash and squish the marshmallow with a brick. There is no brick marshmallow. This is the worst problem with having two different styles of parenting.

One of the other problems with two different parenting styles is children learn to ask the marshmallow parent. As in:

> Child and parents are in a room together. Child walks up to Marshmallow and says, "Can I watch a movie?"
>
> Marshmallow is prepared to say yes but Brick Wall speaks first and says, "No."
>
> Child replies in a snarky voice, "I wasn't talking to you. I was asking Marshmallow."

Which presents a whole new issue about speaking respectfully to each other, but you get the idea.

I know you probably want to know which style is "better." Honestly, neither; you need to fall somewhere in between—authoritative parenting, I believe it is called. You set guidelines and expect your child to follow them but there is room for negotiation. It is based upon respect.

Play Fighting

I tried to limit my boys' exposure to play guns in the house. I refused to buy any for about five years after my first boy (middle child) was born. Then they started to trickle in; first a water gun, then a pop gun, then a Transformers gun. Soon, they were all over.

With these toys came, inevitably, the play shooting. There are only so many times boys will accept they are shooting jello instead of real bullets. It's in the movies and TV shows we watch and the video games as well. Guns are all around us it seems (even though Canada has much more gun regulation than the United States).

Rough housing is another thing I currently struggle with. One day T, who was two at the time, decided D was going to be his pony and climbed up on D's back. Then, out of nowhere, T blurted, "Kill pony." Did I mention he was two at the time?

I just started laughing. I know it was an inappropriate reaction, but it was such an offhand remark that I didn't know what else to do.

In trying to figure out where T got it from, I recalled that the day before it was D's ninth birthday. We had had a small party for him at home. There were only five nine-year-old boys and T. They were running around the house each with a toy gun shooting each other and yelling various phrases which, most likely, included some form of "kill <something>." Kids, being sponges, pick up everything. T was simply parroting what he had heard the day before.

Obviously, I still have a lot of teaching to do when it comes to guns, killing, and the influence of the media and society on my young boys.

Dirty Diapers

When D was born, we had a bad habit of changing his diaper and leaving the dirty one by the couch to put in the garbage later.

At the time, we had a small dog named Ginger. She was a poodle-bichon; a small dog with curly white hair. A rescue, she had some strange mannerisms like peeing on the floor right after she was let in from outside (where she was supposed to do her business).

One thing, thankfully, she never took to was eating from the garbage can; even if it did not have a lid on it. Now if food was left around the house—on a plate or in a closed container—it was fair game.

On one occasion, Ginger came downstairs licking her chops; another annoying habit she had (which we found out later had to do with her teeth rotting) and her white muzzle was somewhat yellowish. We weren't quite sure what it was; we assumed she had found some food we left lying around.

When we went upstairs later, we realized she found a dirty diaper, which she had obviously found quite tantalizing and had decided to slurp up the contents. Ugh. (And you wonder why I never let dogs lick me.)

You think we would have learned our lesson after this happened once but no. It took three or four more of Ginger's snacks and the resulting yellowish muzzle to curb our habit of not putting the diapers directly in the garbage.

Room Cleaning

"Stay in here until your room is clean." That was my way of dealing with my first child's unclean bedroom. Or "clean it up or I will throw it all out." I even bagged it all up once, ready to throw it all away. Did it work? No, of course not. Both of us would become frustrated. Eventually, I'd cave and go in and "direct" her and dictate what to clean. It didn't help in the long run, though.

I started the same routine with my middle child, D. My late husband even did bag up everything and toss it at one point. That got rid of the mess for a bit but then it just came back.

Bribery, threats, "directing," nothing seemed to work then, and it certainly doesn't work now. Then I realized, the problem was me. If I cannot model the behavior, how can I expect my kids to learn?

I'm a slob, a pack rat, a clutter bug, a hoarder; whatever you label it, that's me. I make excuses to justify the mess to myself like, "there's no mold growing so I'm good." It is what it is. I never learned how to clean properly. Clutter and chaos rule my life. My question is, does the chaos create the clutter or does the clutter create the chaos? Oh, J (my late husband) would love that question.

In the book entitled "the life-changing magic of tidying up" by Marie Kondo, she re-iterates the fact that if we don't teach children how to clean they will not learn.

One parenting class I am taking on reducing my yelling (see future chapter) says to break the tasks down into smaller, more manageable chunks like putting away clothes one day, Lego the next, books the next, and so on. Empowering D to take control over his own room, I had him brainstorm his list of tasks which we have posted on his wall. Does it work? When I apply it, yes. Funny thing is, it works for me too. When I have a huge chore to do, I try to break it down into 15-minute tasks; so, the theory works for adults as well.

Throwing things out still provides a challenge for both D and I. When it comes to the artwork coming home from school, I have started taking a picture of it, posting it to Facebook and then discarding the item. This keeps clutter down for sure. And it's starting to work with D as well. Electronically, I can be a packrat without cluttering up my home.

A work in progress; that's my house. I hope by the time my children are ready to move out, I have instilled a sense of cleanliness in them.

Temper Tantrums

Most, if not all, children throw temper tantrums ("patty ons" as I call them). I'm sure every parent has experience with fits of some sort whether it's throwing themselves on the floor, kicking and screaming, or throwing toys around the room in frustration. Tactics that work with one child sometimes do not work the same to diffuse a temper tantrum in another. Personalities differ so solutions have to vary.

Unfortunately for her, my daughter (my first child) was my guinea pig. With her, I would join her on the floor. My goal was to model her behavior. Wait, no it wasn't. It was to embarrass her. I'm not proud of that tactic, even though it was (somewhat) effective.

D was born 14 years after my first child. My solution for him was to never let him get completely overwhelmed to begin with. Did it work? Of course not. We still had issues, but I was more capable to deal with the tantrums. I had to sit with him and calm him down. The school he was at for Kindergarten was an independent one. They taught him to "smell the flowers and blow out the candle" in order to calm down. Honestly, I think I used that technique as often as he did. In fact, I still do.

My latest child can fly off the handle over the smallest thing. The other night, it was because his Ryder figurine (from

Paw Patrol) would not sit "right" on his ATV. That hardly seemed like something to get upset about to me. Despite my trying to fix Ryder so he sat "right," T flipped out. I mean, full on patty on. Ryder got thrown across the bathroom (we were having a bath at the time). I had to get out of the tub, throw on some clothes, and sit and rock T (wrapped in a towel) for about 10 minutes. I had to keep telling him to "smell the flowers, blow out the candle." I modeled the calming technique to him as I rocked. Finally, his crying ceased.

After that, he just wanted to snuggle with me on the couch for another 10 minutes. Then, he popped his head up and said, "I'm good; me go bath now?" We were able to finish his bath (with his brother in the tub with him). Ryder was happily accepted back into the tub sitting on his ATV the exact same way he was in the first place.

I've been doing a lot of reading and research on parenting in the last few years. Apparently, tantrums are a child's way of reaching out for contact or help. One course I'm currently taking suggests if you spend "parent-child" one-on-one time with the child every day, it will help alleviate some of these cries for help (mentally or physically). I've been trying to ensure I do this daily; some days it's harder than others. Time will tell if it becomes effective in eliminating tantrums completely.

Yelling

My speaking voice is naturally very loud; add a topic I'm passionate about, and it gets even louder. When I'm at work, people will often overhear me from a couple cubicles over. It's not intentional; it's just one of my (less desirable) traits.

Add my loud voice to my young boys' communication and our house becomes very noisy at points. That's on a normal day.

Now, add stress to this situation. Despite my best intentions of being a good parent, sometimes I yell at my boys to quiet down or stop fighting. This is not something I'm proud of, but it is a realism in our house. In my defense, I'm human. When stress compounds, I'm a yeller. Former yeller, I should say. I'm working on finding other techniques to reduce the yelling in the house.

A few months ago, I signed up for an online course called Positive Parenting Solutions (https://www.positiveparenting-solutions.com/). I initially balked about paying for a course when I could do the research online myself. Then I realized that reducing the emotional damage I was doing to my boys by yelling was worth *any* amount of money. And so, I signed up. I'm only on session 2 of 9 but the difference has been amazing. The incident the other night with Ryder and the temper tantrum (previous chapter) would never have been handled as well as it was without the course I was taking. Prior to that, I would have yelled at T to stop crying and maybe put him in his room for some quiet time. Recognizing he just needed some mental help and rocking/snuggling with my boy ended the tantrum in record time (yes, 10 minutes is a short tantrum).

I highly recommend if you are having an issue of yelling in your house, take this course. It has been a life saver for my sanity and my boys' emotional well-being.

Child Protective Services

For most of my life, I have lived in rougher neighbourhoods. Places where Child Protective Services (CPS) are called frequently. My experience with CPS is, for the most part, one where I'm making the call about a child in need of help.

In Saskatoon, I once saw a two-year-old child, still in diapers, wander out into the middle of a very busy street. I immediately put on my hazards and scooped the child up. After securing the child, I called CPS. I was told (shockingly) to knock on the doors in the neighbourhood to find the parents.

A little put off, I did so. I still think CPS should have come out and handled the situation.

However, I was on the receiving end one time; it was not a pleasant experience. After we had bought our house in 2008, I was babysitting Z, a friend of mine's (then) one-year-old. It was the first and only time I babysat her; likely because of this experience.

Z had woken up during the night around midnight. My middle son was about the same age. He remained sleeping during this ordeal. I was in the living room (which faces the street), rocking Z and shushing her to try to get her to go back to sleep. Standard action as far as I was concerned.

I noticed a man yelling on the street; given the neighbourhood, I tried to ignore him. He was screaming in my direction and looking at me through the living room window. After contemplating calling the cops, I chose to just continue trying to get Z back to sleep.

Shortly after, there was a knock at the door. Normally I wouldn't open the door that late at night, but I noticed a police cruiser in front of my house. Turns out crazy guy reported me to CPS! A police officer accompanied a social worker, and both were standing outside my door. After letting them inside, I explained what happened. They asked if there were other children in the house and I indicated there was. After showing them to D's room to ensure he was safe, they commented the person who had called in was known to make fraudulent calls, but they had a duty to check it out. It was a totally different response than the one I had received in Saskatoon a decade earlier.

In the meantime, while CPS was still at my house, Z's parents showed up to pick her up. I tried explaining the incident to them. I think they were rather frazzled. They said they understood but since they never asked me to babysit again, I would say that wasn't the case.

I realize CPS is a necessary community service. Unfortunately, it is needed to protect vulnerable children. However, my experiences with the service left much to be desired. Thankfully, that was my last interaction with them to date.

Apologizing

Canadians are known for apologizing unnecessarily. If we bump into someone, we apologize—even if it's not our fault. I'm not sure anyone fully understands this cultural norm. In Toastmasters, one of the members (originally from Ethiopia) actually took time to research this trend of apologizing. In Ontario, they instituted an Apology Act in 2009—the gist of it is that an apology does not constitute an admission of guilt. I thought this member was joking but then I Googled it and it is a real thing: https://www.ontario.ca/laws/statute/09a03. Who knew?

Co-workers have told me several times to stop apologizing (unnecessarily) for things. And then I apologize for apologizing.

Teaching your children to apologize is a natural thing—if they hurt someone else (intentionally or not), for example. While it may not undo the hurt inflicted in its entirety, it is a start—especially for young children just learning how to interact in the world.

As a role model, parents should be expected to apologize to their children when appropriate. Apologizing to your children is not a sign of weakness. It shows you are human. If I do something I am ashamed of or I regret, like yelling, I have no qualms with apologizing.

Sorry, I hope I didn't offend you by suggesting you should apologize. :0)

Hair Dye

House safety 101; when you have small children, keep all cleaning supplies and toxic chemicals out of reach. I secure all these types of chemicals in a high cupboard. However, I never thought of hair dye as a toxic chemical. How wrong I was.

When I was younger, I used to dye my hair a lot. I knew the dye was toxic, therefore I used the proper handling instructions; wear gloves, protect your clothing, discard the bottles in the garbage. I never thought anything of it.

On one occasion, for whatever reason, B decided to pull the used dye bottle out of the garbage and take a huge whiff of it. For those who don't know, there are fumes given off by hair dye and you aren't supposed to inhale them. I walked into the kitchen to find B crying. Through her tears and stammering, I realized what happened. After a huge sniff of the empty dye bottle, B immediately got dizzy and her head started hurting.

Thankfully, my mom was there and knew just what to do. She called the poison control center; I never would have thought of that myself. Thankfully, it was nothing some fresh air couldn't fix.

Oops. And now you know. Don't leave your used dye bottles in a garbage can that is accessible to smaller children.

PART 2

Things I Handled Like a Rock Star!

*T*his section is filled with examples of things I've done as a parent that I am proud of. Strokes of genius—like monster spray and playdough. Fun stories that will make you smile and chuckle; these are the ones I share with other parents if they are experiencing issues such as "monsters" in the closet or under the bed. You can relax your hold on whatever you were grasping during the rough part of this trip; this part of the road is smoother, more scenic, and much more pleasurable.

Mirror Obsession

When my daughter was younger, she would often take forever to get ready for bed; brushing and flossing in the bathroom took a very long time. One night, I sat outside the bathroom and poked my head in after 15 minutes. There my little cutie was standing staring at herself in the mirror on the back of the bathroom door.

"What are you doing?" I inquired.

"Nothing," she replied.

Funny thing is, brushing and flossing took significantly less time after I removed the mirror from the back of the door.

D, my middle boy, likes to stand and stare at himself in the mirror too. Not sure why. His brushing and flossing take a long time as well—mostly because he's procrastinating getting ready for bed.

My youngest son isn't fascinated with mirrors per say but he sure likes to watch videos of himself and examine photographs.

A natural curiosity, I'm sure. At least it was in fascination not disgust. But why does it have to happen at bedtime?

Monster Spray

When she was younger, my daughter was scared to go to bed because she thought the "monsters" would get her. It was a constant fight to put her to bed. My ex-husband and

I brainstormed over what to do. We tried explaining to her that monsters weren't real. We tried getting mad and yelling. Leaving a light on did not help. Nor did leaving the bedroom door open.

One night, we tried using a flashlight to look through her room—under the bed, in the closet and so on. That seemed to work as long as we left the flashlight in her room with her. At least for a while anyway. Unfortunately, it had an unwanted side effect. She played with the light and kept herself up quite late.

We needed another solution. Something to keep monsters at bay, that she could control in her room, and that didn't keep her up all night.

Sometimes strokes of genius come to you from nowhere at all. It came out of the blue. Monster spray. Yes, you read that right. Monster spray.

I found a small spray bottle. I put flat glass stones (the ones you can buy for decoration) in the bottom—about 15 of them. I filled the spray bottle with water, a couple drops of food colouring (so it did not pass for just water, yet it wasn't coloured enough to stain anything) and a couple drops of perfume.

It was brilliant! She could spray the magical concoction everywhere (eliminating monsters on contact). She could keep it close to her bed (and use it whenever she wanted to). And with the stones in the bottom, she could shake it to scare off the monsters who were tricky enough to evade the spray. The bonus was, it didn't keep her awake for long as she couldn't see in the dark to play around.

It was so inspired, I thought I should patent it. But I didn't. Instead I shared it freely with others. It still works.

My middle son, when he was five, started with this same issue. We quickly threw together the concoction and D keeps it by his pillow.

Feel free to use it and pass it on. And by all means, send me a note with your personal story on how it worked.

Nightmares

My middle child, D, started with nightmares when he was five or six. Having the monster spray under my belt, we came up with "good dream spray" which was pretty much monster spray rebranded. Combined with a "good dream pouch" including a spell my late husband came up with, this was exactly what we needed.

Good Dream Pouch Recipe

Small, tie-able cloth bag filled with dry lavender or bits of cotton with a few drops of lavender essential oil. Lavender induces sleepiness and it smells good.

Good Dream Pouch Spell

Light a small candle. Hold the bag close to your heart. Close your eyes. Repeat a short incantation such as, "Goddesses bring good sleep and pleasant dreams to <child's name>. Banish all bad dreams and let my little one sleep well." The exact words are not crucial; only the intent is.

It may not seem like much, but you will be amazed at how well it works with children. Even nine months after J passed, D sleeps with his "good dream pouch."

Playdough Made From Scratch

Sometimes as adults we forget children don't require toys as much as they require your time. Instead of going out to the store to pay (way too much) for play dough, follow this recipe and make your own at home with your child. And the bonus, it's not made of chemicals so if they eat it, they won't get sick!

Ingredients

    2 cups of boiling water
    3 cups of white flour
    1/2 cup salt
    1 tbsp cream of tartar
    3 tbsp vegetable oil
    (optional) Kool-Aid or food colouring for colour

Directions

- Mix ingredients together in a big bowl. Once mixed, pull the dough out and mix it more with your hands. Caution: It may be very hot, so an adult should do this. Let the mixture cool a bit and then play to your heart's content.
- Stores well in zip lock bags or (Tupperware) containers with lids.
- Alternately, you can let it dry and paint it for another activity.

The bonus of this playdough is that, while it takes time, it is a quick activity your kids can participate in—both making it and playing with it after. Fun!

Slime

My youngest son likes to watch YouTube and came across this recipe for slime. It can be varied. When you work it long enough, it becomes more like a putty than slime (parents will appreciate this because it's less messy to clean up).

Ingredients

    Bottle of glue (white, clear, glitter, whatever you prefer)

Half a cup of water
One tsp Borax
Glitter (optional)
Food colouring (optional)
Two bowls
Storage container

Directions

- ∞ Pour glue into a bowl. Add glitter and/or food colouring as desired. Mix.
- ∞ In a separate bowl, mix water with Borax. Stir well.
- ∞ Transfer small amounts of the Borax/water solution into the glue. Start with a tablespoon. Mix. Add more water until it's fairly slimy.
- ∞ Using your hands, keep mixing and it will eventually turn into a more putty like substance.
- ∞ Slime will keep for months as long as you store it in a sealed storage container.

To remove from clothing or textured surfaces, apply vinegar and rub gently. Launder clothing normally. If it's on a couch or rug, just scrub it off. Any lingering vinegar smell will dissipate over time.
Enjoy!

Christmas Presence

This chapter was written in 2014—D was five and T wasn't born yet.

"Mommy, I want a toy kitty for Christmas." "Mommy, tell Santa I want a remote-control monster truck for Christmas." How many of you have heard these statements from kids around Christmas? My son "only" wants a toy kitty (even though we have a real one) and a remote-control monster truck (even though he has several different versions).

Personally, I'm sick of him getting toys—for Christmas, for birthdays, just because. We have more toys than one little boy could *ever* need. And yet, he wants the newest and best, shiny toys. Well, he wants any toys really. They don't have to be new as long as they are new to him. That being said, D also has no trouble giving away toys to those less fortunate (usually as a negotiation for a new toy).

And my little boy isn't the only one suffering from the "I wants." In today's commercialized version of Christmas, we are creating monsters in ourselves and others. How many deaths were a result of Black Friday this year. Anyone? http://www.blackfridaydeathcount.com/ reports seven deaths and ninety injuries. I watched YouTube fights in Walmart over packages of paper. *Paper.*

This year, I read an article in the Huffington Post by Christella Morris—The gift of not giving a thing. http://www.huffingtonpost.com/christella-morris/the-gift-of-not-giving-a-thing_b_4236040.html I was so inspired, I vowed not to buy any more presents. I have committed to providing "presence" this year instead of "presents." So, how am I going to do this? Great question!

#1—If we must buy presents, we will limit the price to $40. If a gift will cost more, that person has to find others to pitch in on it. Or better yet, shop *after* Christmas and get all the deals. *Everything* goes on sale after Christmas. Even turkeys. And who is to say Christmas dinner has to be *on* Christmas? It's the spirit and intention that matters. We are having a winter solstice supper on December 21 and Christmas supper on January 5.

#2—Make presents. We like to give presents so why not dedicate the 12 months between Christmases to make something? Next year, I'm crocheting my honey a red and white poncho (he's a Stampeder's fan). Any hobby can be taken up to make a present—baking, needlepoint, painting, wood working, post carding, etc.

#3—Make ornaments. This year, we are not putting commercial ornaments on our tree, only those that are homemade. My daughter made a lot when she was younger, and I kept them. Last year, we made popcorn strings (and found out the history behind them). This year, we painted little wooden ornaments we bought at Canadian Tire.

#4—Spend time with your children. Like the author of this article, make family time key—no matter what activity you choose to participate in. Going to Christmas events—like the Royal Canadian Air Force Concert last night, Lights Across Canada tomorrow night, CEP (Communications, Energy and Paperworkers Union of Canada) Annual Kids' Christmas Party on Sunday—or even volunteering to sing carols at a couple senior's homes on Christmas Day or taking a shift at the Food Bank. The opportunities are endless. And they don't just have to be at Christmas time. Plenty of worthwhile organizations look for volunteers all year round—SaskTel Pioneers, Bright Eyes Dog Rescue, Heritage Community Association—to name a few.

Wouldn't it be nice if, instead of material things, we gave our children our presence? This is something I think everyone can give. Instead of a new toy, buy (or make) a certificate redeemable for a day at the zoo or the Science Center. Learn something new, like painting, pottery, or dancing. Take them to that new movie they want to see or the local play place (even if it is at McDonald's).

P R E S E N C E not P R E S E N T S ... what a concept!

Family Time

With our first child, my ex-husband and I had a rule you had to be home every day for at least an hour to visit. This usually constituted supper at home every evening. We justified this by saying it was our family time to re-connect. Now, it may appear to be a rule for the sake of a rule, but I believe regular interaction is crucial in any relationship, especially for families. Parents were also expected to be home for supper every day. Now that I think about it, it makes sense as to why I make so much effort now with my younger boys to ensure I am home at supper time. Interesting, because I never realized the connection until just now as I was writing this.

After B moved out, she continued to visit us once or twice a week. After J passed, this became three or four times a week. She says she misses us. I think she just needs someone to take care of. First it was my mom. When my mom went to a senior's home, it was J (his cancer diagnosis led me to decide to put Mom into a nursing home). Now that they have both passed, I think she's adopted me as the next logical person to take care of.

With the boys growing up so quickly, I want to ensure I spend adequate family time with them. These family memories are all they will have left once I'm gone. One on one time is important but so is family time. Nothing can replace that.

Nickelback

My daughter, B, has always been an energetic child. She is full of life. She thrives on music and enjoys many genres. I am a HUGE Nickelback fan and so B has grown to enjoy the band almost as much as me. It was announced in October 2003 that Nickelback would be coming to Regina the following January.

Of course, I really wanted to go. I awoke the day the tickets went on sale and headed down to the Cornwall mall an hour before they went on sale. Anticipation of attaining these tickets was high; that was until I saw the lineup. My heart began palpitating; my palms started sweating. I was prancing back and forth from one foot to the other. The line was so long. Should I go to a different Ticketmaster—perhaps at the Casino? Would I get tickets? I hoped I would. Tickets went on sale at 10 a.m. but the Shoppers I was at was experiencing technical difficulties, so they took an extra 10 minutes to start selling the tickets. The line moved like molasses in January (sloowwwlllllyyyyy). I thought for sure I would not get tickets; there must have been 100 people ahead of me. Finally, my turn came. I asked for 3 tickets together and crossed my fingers. The woman turned to me and said, "I have 3 tickets in section PP" to which I eagerly replied, "I'll take them." I breathed a sigh of relief especially when I heard the salesperson say to the person behind me "We are now sold out." I had managed to attain the tickets. My daughter would be really excited! Never mind that, *I* was really excited.

I told B that I had gotten tickets for Auntie Tasha and I to go see Nickelback. The disappointment rang clear on her face ... until I said she was coming too. Her eyes lit up; she talked about it for months after that. "I'm going to Nickelback," she would proudly announce to anyone and everyone who would listen to her: complete strangers, friends, cashiers, whomever. The looks of jealousy she got from some people did not deter her.

My daughter awoke in anticipation on the big day. As we looked out the frost-covered window, her mood changed; her eyes drooped down, ready to fill with tears. A fluffy white blanket of snow greeted our eyes. A blanket that went half way up the side of the car. How were we going to get to the concert? We both had been looking forward to this day since I bought the tickets.

She turned to me and vocalized the same question I was wondering, "Mom, how are we going to get there?"

"Well, B," I replied with disappointment in my own voice, "the concert will likely be cancelled." After all, the Saskatoon concert the previous night had been poorly attended. Surely this one would be cancelled. The look of dismay on B's face was clear.

We turned on the radio and listened intently for any news of the concert. Hours passed with no word. I called Ticketmaster—they said they did not know if it was still on. Finally, an announcement came on. Our faces both lit up as they confirmed the concert was still on. Now we just had to figure out how we were going to get there.

My friend was already on the bus from Medicine Hat, AB. In addition to determining how to get to the concert, I had to figure out how we would get to the bus depot to pick her up. With determination in my eyes, I announced that if all else failed, we would walk to the concert. It was only 20 blocks away but it sure would be a long walk in two feet of snow. Hours passed. Around 4 p.m., I heard a very loud engine outside. I looked out the front window to see what all the ruckus was.

And what to my wondering eyes did appear? A beautiful yellow coloured grader switching gear ...

Unbeknownst to me, our front street was high priority on snow removal as it led to the Neil Balkwill Centre. I rushed out to move the car, so he could grade right up to the sidewalk.

Our problem was solved! Both of us danced around the house in jubilation chanting, "We're going to Nickelback." My friend arrived shortly before the concert, I was at the bus station to pick her up.

We arrived at the concert at 7 p.m. in time to hear both opening bands. When Nickelback came out, the crowd roared. It was deafening. The music pumped, and we screamed until our throats were sore. The pyrotechnics caused us to jump every single time they went off. Our bodies pounded from the bass for two glorious hours.

After the concert, as we were walking out to the car, still vibrating from the excitement, B turned to me and declared, "That eff-ing rocked!" Tasha and I burst out laughing. Ah kids, they have the perfect way of summing things up, because in truth, I had to agree. "That eff-ing rocked!"

Washroom Usage

When B was around two or three and was just learning how to use the potty, there were times she had to go (and she had to go right then and there). We were on a walk to a local park one day when she indicated she had to go, so, we walked into a local sub shop. Now I made sure the shop had no sign up about washrooms being for customer use only; I will respect those.

However, when we walked past the counter, the employee asked, "What can I get you?"

When I replied, "Nothing, we're just using the washroom."

He stated, "Sorry, washrooms are for customers only."

"It's for her," I stated, indicating my young girl.

The employee started to argue.

"Then put up a sign," I retorted as I took B into the washroom and let her pee.

I get the premise of not wanting a bunch of non-paying people to use a washroom because it costs the business money—but put up a sign—or bend the rules for a child.

After I left, I thought maybe I should have let her squat and pee just outside the restaurant to prove a point. :0)

Some women take an insane amount of time in the washroom. I've never understood why. The line-ups for women's washrooms are often very long, no matter how many toilets they have.

Case in point. As a young adult, I partook in pub crawls—one of them was right before the Calgary Stampede. At every bar we stopped at, women would proceed to the washroom first thing. The lineup had 25 to 30 women in it and it took a good 30 minutes to get through the line despite there being 10 toilets in the washroom. After the first couple stops, women in the lineup would chant, "Pee and go. Pee and go." Though it never made the women go any faster, it occupied the drunk ladies in the line.

When we were at the Nickelback concert (previous chapter), B indicated she had to go to the washroom just before the band was coming on stage. The women's washroom line was crazy, so I covered her eyes and marched her into the men's room. I put her in the stall and stood with my head against the door, trying to ignore all the men using the urinals. After she was done, we skipped washing our hands and just walked out. Ironically, the men didn't seem to care. No one said anything to us.

Recently, there has been a lot of controversy about gender identification and washroom usage. Personally, I don't understand why anyone would care what the person in the stall next to them has for genitalia. Just use the washroom and go.

There is a semi-valid argument about men using the women's washroom, in particular, where men may take advantage of women in this situation, however, this happens in public areas already; I don't think men using the women's washrooms would contribute to this issue.

Recently, I've noticed that in a lot of the new schools (and workplaces), they have started to use genderless, single washrooms. That makes me quite happy actually because no one should be bothered by what's under your pants when you have to use the facilities. Plus, that gets rid of any bullying that might occur in the multi-use washrooms.

North Americans have too much time on their hands when they worry about who has what, where, and why when using the washroom. Just pee and go. Say it with me, "Pee and go!"

Sex Ed

B (Grade 1): "I know what sex is."
Me: "Oh?"
B: "It's when two people get naked and kiss."
Oh, the innocence of youth. What can you do but chuckle?

Planned Parenthood Classes

Planned Parenthood held a summer camp program the year my daughter was 12. As sex education is something our kids need to learn—whether through parents or through school—I decided to send her to the camp. They had girlie-type workshops in the afternoon—like how to make homemade lip balm. I thought B would enjoy it. In fact, I also sent my niece (11 years old), who was living with us.

One day, after class, I was in the process of making supper. I was cutting up vegetables with a large kitchen knife. B, my daughter, nonchalantly walked into the kitchen and proceeded to tell me about her day.

"They gave me a condom today," she announced.

"Oh?" I responded. Thinking she wouldn't really have any use for it, I asked, "Can I have it?"

"No. I used it," she stated, matter-of-factly.

I paused my cutting. Minor panic setting in as a variety of notions flew rapidly through my brain. After I set the knife down gently, I turned slowly towards her and inquired, "You used it?"

"Yeah, we took it out of the package, put it on the tips of our fingers, and rolled it up our arm. It went all the way up to here!" She made the motion of putting the condom on the end of her fingers and showed it went all the way up to the top of her arm (near her shoulder).

Relief started to pour through me as she continued, "So, if a guy says it doesn't fit, you know they are lying!"

I burst out laughing. Whoever came up with that was brilliant!

And my (shy) niece, who would never have dreamed of ever talking about anything like this with me (or her mom) piped up and said, "You know what else Aunty?"

"What?" I answered between fits of laughter.

"If you tickle your arm with a feather [with the condom on], you can totally feel it. So, if a guy says he can't feel anything with it on, you know he's lying."

Yeah, these nuggets were precious; the class was worth its weight in gold. These were the two wisest things these two adolescents could ever learn. I sent a note to the organizers and praised them on their ingenuity. These lessons were sure to never be lost.

Planned Parenthood Summer Education programs rock!

Sex Ed—New Generation

My late husband's youngest teenage son was living with us for a few months. Being brought up by someone else, he wasn't aware of how open and honest I could be about pretty much anything.

Upon him relaying to J and I that he had a girlfriend, I casually mentioned there was a tin of condoms under the bathroom sink. As his mouth dropped open in shock, I smiled and told him to take as many as he needed.

Having become a parent just before I turned 20, I now understand the need to use protection when you are sexually active. It's quite important, for both boys and girls, to have access to sex education. They need to protect themselves from sexually transmitted infections (STIs) and from becoming a parent when they do not want to be.

Unfortunately, the onus is usually put on the girls to prevent pregnancy. I instilled this in my daughter and I intend to teach my boys, as well, because I think it's important both sides of a relationship have the information they need to remain safe and prevent unplanned pregnancies.

Road Trips

"Road trip?"

"You mean like spring vackay? Let's all go! Road trip. AAAEEEIII!" (Legally Blonde movie quote.)

This little ditty is what we often say when our family starts a vacation together. The first time I screeched it, my young son looked at me like I was crazy but now he says it just for fun.

Road trips are the staple of our vacations. We often plan a little route which includes going through Alberta. We pack up the family. And we leave ample time for stops. It is important to leave extra travel time when you have younger children. They tend to get bored very fast. You will want to stop every hour or so when they are younger, say under age five. If you do not stop frequently, you run the risk of losing your mind. Literally. Children are not meant to sit for long periods of time. So, pull the car over and let them stretch their little legs. Your trip will be immensely more enjoyable.

That is only the first bit of advice for road trips. The next bit is to ensure you are driving only five to six hours a day total. That five to six hours may take you nine hours, in reality. Find a hotel that has a pool or find a nice campground. Your children will have fun anywhere. Try to find something else fun to do where you are staying. For example, when we were travelling from Regina to Calgary, we chose to stop in Medicine Hat and stayed at their campground. It was quite a nice venue with trails to run for the older people and a playground for the younger ones.

Breaking up a long road trip into bite-size travel pieces will make the experience all the more memorable. I often find the adults enjoy the side trips as much as the children do. Maybe more. (Because they get to keep their sanity.)

Our road trips have included trips to Edmonton, Calgary, Victoria, Ontario, and Prince Albert. The shorter ones could be done in a week, but the longer ones took roughly three weeks.

Set a goal for the trip. When we travelled to Victoria, not only was our goal to remain stress free, we committed to eating ice cream every day. We almost succeeded; we forgot a couple days but that's okay.

Bring things to do! Those kiddos can only watch Paw Patrol so many times (though at least 10 times more than adults could withstand). Colouring books, stickers and blank paper, little cars/transformers/figurines. Anything goes. If one of your children is a little older, they can often occupy the younger one(s) with a couple of toys.

Snacks are imperative. Healthy snacks, even more so. While stopping at gas stations and convenience stores is a nice break from driving, it becomes very expensive—both in terms of money and health. Children may enjoy the extra sugar binge because sugar lights up the pleasure centers of their brains (similar to how cocaine does) but they have sugar highs (hyperactivity) and then they crash afterwards. If you have ever overdone sugar or junk food, you know what I'm talking about.

Be flexible. The plan is a guideline; it is not set in stone. (Kind of like parenting.) If you planned to stop in certain places at certain times but the kids need a break sooner (or—surprise!—they are napping) then change it up. Hotel rooms can even be changed last minute. Most let you cancel the same day until 6 p.m. without any penalty.

Try to look for the positives—even when a series of events threatens to make your sunny day a thunderstorm. On our road trip to Victoria, BC, the first day had me doubting the sanity of the trip.

We planned to leave Regina around noon so our littlest one, who was one at the time, would nap. Our *plan* was to travel to Brooks, AB that day; a little longer than our five-hour per day limit on travel time.

Unfortunately, T *hated* car rides. My other two kids loved car rides; the motion would lull them to sleep. I remember driving B around Saskatoon at 4 a.m. to get her to sleep (though she'd wake up right after we stopped). Anyway, T freaked out right outside Regina. It was that crying that nothing can soothe. My late husband, J, crawled into the back of the van to try to calm him. We pulled over, so I could try to calm him. We decided to keep driving in the hopes he would fall asleep. Two hours later, he (finally) did. It was a long, grueling afternoon.

We decided to pull over in Medicine Hat for a break some time later. Supper had already been eaten and was digesting in our tummies. While taking the off-ramp towards the Walmart, a huge noise reverberated through the van and it pulled to one side. I knew immediately we had blown a tire. I pulled over just past the set of lights at the bottom of the off ramp. J said he would swap out the flat for the spare tire on the car while the boys and I went over to the Tim Horton's across the field. Ironically, we call our spare tire a "donut" in North America; to try to keep the mood light, I joked about going to get donuts while J put the "donut" on the car. About 30 minutes later, we were back on the road. It was now around 7 p.m. We considered staying overnight in Medicine Hat but as it was past 6 p.m., we would still have had to pay for the hotel in Brooks. So, we pressed on.

The spare tire had a manufacturer's recommended speed of 80 km/hr. Even though it added time to our journey, we chose to maintain this speed as we did not have a spare for the spare. All the tire shops were already closed when we were in Medicine Hat.

An hour later, J looked down at the dash when he saw a light flicker on. Low fuel. In the kerfuffle of swapping out the flat tire, we neglected to check how much gas was left in the tank. Dammit! We were exactly halfway between Brooks and Medicine Hat with no gas station in sight. Turning around was not an option. I pulled out my cell phone and Googled nearby gas stations. What luck, there was a town about 5 km off the main highway.

As we drove down the main street (if it can be called that) of this little hick town, we could not find the gas station. Pulling over to inquire with someone walking their dog, we were dismayed to hear the local gas station had closed a couple years back. But there was another town about 15 km further off the highway that had one. Whew. We drove there, praying we wouldn't run out of gas on the way.

As we pulled up to the station, we realized it had closed 20 minutes earlier. Of all the luck. This day could not get any worse. Or could it?

Driving back to the main highway, we contemplated our options. We could chance driving to Brooks and running out of gas completely or we could pull over and call CAA (Canadian Automobile Association—emergency roadside assistance program). I had heard somewhere that with a fuel-injected vehicle, such as ours was, you should never run the engine out of gas completely as there is extra priming that needs to be done. Now I do not profess to be a mechanic, but I did not want to risk potentially having to do more to the vehicle than just get gas. It was now nearing 9 p.m.

CAA it was. Upon calling them, we were informed it would be at least an hour before someone could get to us. I hung up the phone and started crying. Through my blubbering, I told J we should just turn around and go home; I couldn't handle a full three weeks of days like today. I was still sobbing when

I heard a small voice from my six-year-old in the back seat, "Mommy, look at the beautiful sunset."

I stopped and looked ahead of us and saw the glorious sight. Through the tears, I looked back at my son and told him what a beautiful sunset it was and that I was so glad he could still find the positives in a day like the one we were having.

That little insight from my wonderful, thoughtful son changed our outlook on the day. We *did* have things to be thankful for: CAA had someone to send to us; my husband's foresight and planning had led him to purchase a CAA membership before we left; and we were starting a road trip that could only get better.

It was just after 10 p.m. when the CAA driver showed up and rescued us. He put $20 worth of gasoline in our van (another positive—this was covered by our CAA membership). Their policy, he told us, was to follow us to the nearest gas station (which happened to be in Brooks—our final destination for that day) to ensure we got there without requiring further assistance. Even though we explained we had to drive 80 km/hr because of the spare tire, he insisted on making sure we got there. I still don't know if this was an actual policy or if he made it up to ensure we were not stranded with two small children in the middle of nowhere.

Upon arriving in Brooks and filling the vehicle up with gas, we pooled our cash and gave the pittance to the driver as thanks for his assistance; I don't remember how much it was, but I know it was a measly amount that did not even begin to compensate him for his time.

We thanked him profusely and sent him on his way back to his family while we settled in at the hotel for the night. It was now after 11 p.m.

The next morning, we started the day refreshed and the rest of the three-week trip went swimmingly. Well, except for a minor trip to the ER (hospital emergency room) in Victoria halfway through our trip when J managed to sprain his ankle hiking while the kids and I vegged on the beach. Imagine my surprise when I got a call from a stranger telling me my husband was being transported via ambulance to the hospital in Victoria.

A plethora of memories were made on that trip (before J got diagnosed with cancer).

It is possible to plan and execute a family road trip even with small children in the car. Plan short breaks every couple of hours; pack snacks and things to do in the car; limit total driving per day to less than five hours; work in activities along the way; and above all, remember your overall goal you set for the trip—whatever it might be. Finally, even when you're driving on fumes with a donut on your car; focus on the positives—you had a spare, the car is running, you have CAA and the sunset *is* beautiful.

Who's Everyone?

Life is so unfair. Especially when you are a child.

Who hasn't heard, "But Mom, *everyone* else is doing it!"

The Path to Perfection

Back when B was in Grade 8 (granted, not quite a teenager but close enough) she wanted to wear makeup. At the time we had a strict policy (aka a rule for the sake of rules) she did not need makeup until she was 16. And so, the convincing started.

(whiny) "But Mom, *everyone* else gets to wear makeup at school."

"Like who?" I'd ask.

(small, meek voice) "McKayla."

"And who else?"

(small, meek voice) "McKayla."

Eventually when she was 14 she got to wear makeup to school. Yes, I caved but I couldn't have her the *only* one not wearing makeup. LOL!

Having a cell phone was the next drama at our house. Of course, the, "But Mom, *everyone* else gets to have a cell phone," reasoning would not work. But I refused to get her a cell phone because my ex-husband and I had just gotten one and we firmly believed a teenager didn't need one. So, new strategy: she nagged. And nagged. And nagged. And she tried persuading, "Well Mom, if I had a cell phone, I could have called you or you could have gotten a hold of me." And then Nana started nagging on B's behalf (I'm not sure if that was planned or not). Eventually, we caved. Not because B wanted it but because we saw the "value" of her having one with all the time she spent away from home.

Peer pressure is a real thing, though. I know plenty of people, even adults, who do things because others do. Never underestimate the power of stupid people in large groups. I'm a lot more flexible now when my child comes to me with a want and a good justification for it. Rather than just stating, "Everyone else …"

Grounding Revamped

I remember when grounding meant you were sent to your room; it was not fun. There was nothing really to do except stare at the wall. That was a long time ago, though. When my daughter was young, being sent to her room was actually enjoyable. She could play, and no one bothered her. So, grounding as a disciplinary measure did not work with my daughter until we came up with an innovative solution.

"Grounding" would now consist of being banned from all electronics. This included the television, the computer, and, later on, the cell phone. The look of horror on my daughter's face when I first suggested this was priceless. I knew I had hit her where it hurts, so to speak. And it worked.

It works with my middle boy too. If I threaten to ban him off my cell phone (he plays games on it), he will usually do as I ask him. Sad, but true.

Changing up the rules of grounding. Brilliant.

In My Days …

I remember one supper out at Red Lobster, J and I had both purposely left our cell phones at home. While we were waiting for supper to be brought to the table, D asked if he could play on my phone. I told him I hadn't brought it. He asked J if he could play on his phone, but J had left his phone home as well. D was flabbergasted. He could not imagine making it through a whole hour without a phone in his hand.

When I mentioned to D in conversation that we didn't even have cell phones when I was younger, he did not believe me. I had to show him pictures of the phones we used to use—with the cord and all.

Yes, imagine the horror of being tethered (literally) to the phone only at your house in one specific three-foot area. No caller ID to tell us who was calling, no answering machines to tell us who called, and no way to move around with a mobile phone. How did we ever live without our cell phones?

There was a cute video on Facebook of a mom who asked her son to use a rotary phone. A rotary phone is an old phone with a cord between the handle and the body of the phone. A cord existed between the base and the wall too. The base of the phone had a dial on it that you stuck your fingers in and rotated to call. (Back then, you only had to dial four or seven numbers.) Here's an image for those who are visual:

It was hilarious watching this boy, who had never seen one of these phones, try to use it. He really tried. He put his fingers in the dial and rotated it. All 10 numbers in a row. Before he picked up the handle. (You had to pick up the handle first and then dial the number.) I could understand why he was having trouble, especially seeing he had not grown up with this type of phone. You can still purchase these phones, but they don't work on our land lines (that's what we call home phones now even though the cord may only go from the base to the wall jack) any more—Canada no longer supports the dial tone rotary phones require.

Some day in the future, I'm sure the same boy will be watching his grandchild struggle with one of our modern cell phones and laughing as they try to use it.

It's hard to imagine not having a cell phone now. I know I'm lost when I forget mine at home. In my short lifetime, we've gone from wired land lines only used at one location to portable wireless cell phones that even our kids are becoming dependent on.

Spaced Out Children

When I talk about "spaced out" children, I am not talking about drugged children but rather about leaving long gaps of time between your children. LOL!

My daughter was 14 when I decided to have my second child. At first, she was excited. She even wanted to be in the delivery room. However, I decided I didn't want anyone else in the delivery room other than my ex-husband. Once the baby came home, my daughter realized how much work her brother actually was. She decided she never wanted to have children. (Which was good at the time.) Spacing out your children is great birth control for young adults.

My third child entered the world when my daughter was 20 and my first son was six. She thought I was crazy for starting again so late in life. After T was born, my daughter started thinking about having her own family. Then she decided it would be "freaky" to have a child the same age as her sibling. She has procrastinated a little longer. Again, this is a good thing as at 40 I was not ready to become a grandparent.

Having children so far apart though can be challenging; as you grow older, you tire more easily. You forget how much energy a three-year-old has. Some days, *I* need the nap more than he does.

Ask the Other Parent

Children learn very quickly that people are different; you will get different answers if you ask different people the same question. My oldest figured this out quite quickly. If she didn't get the answer she wanted, she would go ask the other parent.

Child: "Can I watch a movie?"

Mom: "Not right now, go play."

Mom goes about her business, cleaning or whatever. A short while later, Mom walks into the living room and her child is watching a movie. "I thought I said 'no' to watching a movie?"

Child: "I asked Dad and he said 'yes'."

In all fairness, Dad didn't know Mom had said no so it's not a blatant attempt to undermine Mom's decision. How to solve this issue, though? It was unacceptable to pit parents against each other.

Our solution was to take away whatever it was our child asked for, for the entire day. In this case, no TV or movies for the rest of the day. That behavior got nipped in the bud very quickly and our child quit doing this.

High School Trip

When B was in Grade 12 she came home with a brochure about S-Trip, a company that arranges trips for various schools across North America.

My initial thought was, "Hell, no!" I envisioned all the things that could go wrong on an all-inclusive trip to another country with a bunch of teenagers. Drinking and sex being two of the major issues for me. Having sex while drinking—even worse.

Using my level-headed, rational mom brain, instead of blurting out my first reaction, I simply stated that of course she could go. If she came up with the money to pay for it herself. I mean, how was a teenage girl, with an active social life, going to come up with a couple thousand dollars to go on a trip. I was in my late thirties at the time and I had never managed to save up money to travel anywhere outside continental North America.

As I chuckled mentally about my ingenuity, B signed up immediately, committing to raise the full amount prior to the deadline established by the company. We talked at length about her forfeiting all the money she paid into it if she did not complete the fundraising goal.

Fundraising began. B saved money when she got paid from her job at Tim Horton's. She forfeited nights out with her friends. She asked for money instead of gifts for her birthday. An ad in the online classifieds for bottle donations brought in a couple hundred dollars. One of the donors collected bags of bottles in her apartment building because she was so happy B was fundraising for herself to go on this trip. This lady told me she was glad to see I wasn't just paying for B's trip—that B was actively working towards paying for it herself.

A little unintended consequence of this experience was that I, inadvertently, was teaching my daughter (more) responsibility and goal setting. Yes, she raised the full amount herself. In the time allotted. I was proud (and a little scared).

My late husband was really into self-defense. We had talked about our concerns with B going on this trip with all the drinking that would be going on. My daughter is not only intelligent, she is very beautiful. She often attracts (unwanted) attention from males. I was concerned with her safety, so J suggested to B that she and her friends should learn some basic self-defense skills before they went.

B gathered a couple of her girl friends and over the next few days, J taught them some basics about how to protect themselves. I watched them and learned a few things myself. When someone is coming at you and grabs ahold of you, your instinct is what? To pull away. To try to get free. To flee. When the person is bigger and stronger than you, this is ineffective. Instead, you should take your space and move in towards them, get into the other person's bubble. As they move away, take more space, and more. Keep getting into the other person's face. It throws them off and usually they will let you go.

Armed with this self-defense knowledge, my girl flew off to Cuba for a week.

Upon her return, I asked her how the trip was.

"Mom, did you know it would all be about drinking and sex?"

Um. Yes. But I didn't say that. We talked at length about how she and her friends isolated themselves a bit by staying in a quieter part of the resort. They drank, but not excessively. And they never had to use their self-defense lessons, which I was happy about.

This learning experience wasn't just B's alone. I learned a lot, too. About how to support my child's decision, even if I don't agree with it. That's a very tough (and important) lesson for any parent.

If you teach your children the lessons they need instead of trying to protect them from the world, they will learn responsibility and how to cope in the world. Honestly, that's all I can hope for as a parent. To know I taught my kids how to become successful adults.

Mama Bear

My daughter nicknamed me "Mama Bear" and I'm fairly confident it had to do with this particular occasion. I think she was 12 at the time.

It was July or August and Hedley was playing at Summer Invasion in our town (before the band's big controversy with the #MeToo movement). My daughter and I decided to go listen to the band as we both liked their music. My friend,

Tasha, was with us. B was dressed in shorts and a T-shirt, typical attire for a hot summer day.

Before I continue, I have to clarify something. My daughter is very beautiful; she doesn't think she is, but I know she is. And it's not just because I'm her mom that I think that. Over the years, I have noticed men (grown men might I add) and boys gawking at her. I went to the bar with her a few times and observed the males watching her (with no shame). She was offered free drinks; many young men asked her to dance. Even when she isn't trying, she attracts (unwanted) male attention.

On this particular day, I was lagging a bit behind B as I was talking to Tasha. All of a sudden, four boys jumped out and surrounded B. I didn't hear what they were saying but I started going towards them. Just as suddenly as they appeared, they departed. I wasn't sure what it was about, and B said she wasn't, either.

I told her those boys were lucky they took off when they did as I was just turning into "Mama Bear" mode—like when a mama bear and a cub are separated and someone or something gets in between them. Everyone with any sense of self-preservation knows to never, ever get between a mama bear and her cub.

The rest of the day was uneventful. We enjoyed the concert and returned home safely. And so, I became and still am referred to, with affection, by my daughter as "Mama Bear."

Tattoos

Oh, the taboo of getting a tattoo. There was a strict "no tattoos until you are 18" rule in our house; another example of a rule for the sake of rules. It wasn't a safety thing to my ex; it was a "because I said so" rule.

My daughter broached the subject of tattoos before she was 16. Her dad was dead set against her getting a tattoo. Nana (her dad's mom) made it quite clear to B, in no uncertain terms, that tattoos were the devil. Nana went on and on and on about why people would want tattoos. She didn't understand the appeal. She didn't have any tattoos; and her son certainly didn't have any. Until she passed away.

When my ex-husband and I separated, my daughter broached the subject of tattoos again. She needed parental permission at the tattoo place because she was under 18.

She had a very clear idea of what she wanted for her tattoo. We discussed it at length. And I signed the permission form. The only caveat was she had to pay for it herself. So once again she saved and when she had enough money, she got her tattoo.

For a year or so, she tried to hide her tattoo from her dad and her Nana. Eventually they found out. I don't know what the first reaction was. I know neither were happy with me for letting her get the tattoo so early.

Then she turned 18. Now she was able to get as many tattoos as she wanted, without anyone's permission. She went ahead and got several more. I recall the first time she came home with a new tattoo and I remarked I hadn't signed the permission form. Then I remembered, she was all grown up and capable of making these decisions for herself now. She is still adding to her collection and I find they are actually quite nice.

Fast forward five years or so. Now her dad even has a couple of tattoos on his forearms. I'm sure if B hadn't gotten hers first, he would not have ever gotten them.

In fact, even I caved and got a couple. The smaller ones on each of my ankles did not hurt much. After J passed, I got a couple more; one on my wrist and one on my calf. The latter was larger and it hurt a lot. It is a tree with my kids' names in the roots. There's a howling wolf by the tree for J and a dove flying off the tree for my mom. The artist did a phenomenal job of it, but I think that's it for me. Personally, I'd rather give birth again without anesthesia than get anymore ink; it hurts less. *evil grin*

Making Responsible Choices

As a parent, some of the wisdom doled out to me was regarding "natural consequences." There are consequences to every choice and action; some are direct or "natural" consequences, and some are indirect. An example of a "natural consequence" would be getting a sunburn because one did not apply sunscreen while spending time outside, whereas an indirect consequence might be your car broke down because you overspent on luxuries (and thus did not have your engine maintenance done).

When I was in my early twenties, my ex-husband and I had a couple of irresponsible adults in our life. People that did things I never wanted my kids to do and, as a result, should have been left to deal with their "natural consequences." Let's call these folks R and Jr.

R liked to call us early in the morning to get us to pick him up from the drunk tank at the police station. Luckily for him, my ex-husband picked up the phone. I know if I had, he would have gotten an earful from me about the consequences of drunk driving. And I would have let him stay there the night. Natural consequences to idiotic behavior.

And then my younger brother, Jr, called one night to get us to pick him up from the police station. For whatever reason when he went out that night, he chose to park his car in some crazy manner partially up on top of the curb. He then had gone out drinking. Upon returning to his car, he decided to smoke some weed (marijuana).

A nearby police officer pulled up behind him. Jr put the bag of weed between his legs. Not a great hiding place as it subsequently fell onto the ground as Jr was asked to get out of the car. Not only was Jr going to be driving under the influence of alcohol, which, in itself, is a criminal offence, he was in possession of a substance that was, at the time, illegal. Double whammy.

Again, if it had been me who picked up the phone, Jr would have dealt with his consequences without any intervention from me. Fortunately for him, my ex answered and went to pick Jr up.

As my daughter was growing up, we had many conversations about drinking and driving. I instilled in her the fact she could call me anytime (day or night) to pick her up from anywhere. No questions asked. No lecture. Whether she was drunk, high, or just in trouble—I would pick her up. *If* she called me before she made an irresponsible choice. But if she chose to call me after the police had picked her up, she would remain in their custody and live with the choices she made.

Thankfully, my daughter continues to be very responsible. She's even been my designated driver from time to time.

Saying No

How many of you have had an elementary school child who comes up to you at the end of the day and asks, "Can so-and-so come over?" I don't know about you, but when my young child did this to me, I always felt overwhelmed and pressured to say yes. Often, I could see the other parent struggling with what to say as well.

That's when I picked up a copy of the book "How to talk so your children will listen and how to listen so your children talk." One of the things this book says is to minimize the word "no." One of the suggestions it had was to say, "Yes. Let's pick a time next week." Amazingly, this worked with my daughter and the other parent looked at me in gratitude as we picked a date for a visit.

Learning to say no in a positive manner with an alternate solution saved my sanity more than once.

Jobs

At 15 years old, my daughter decided she wanted to get a job. This was not an idea I embraced as I had a job when I was young and I found it interfered a lot with school. I did not want the same thing for her. But after a lot of persistence from her, I reluctantly agreed.

My only condition was that it didn't interfere with her school. That however, proved to be impossible. Not only was my daughter taking a full load of classes, she was on the cheerleading team, she had a full social calendar, and now she was adding a part-time job.

Again, I had to examine my motives of why I had the rule that it should not interfere with her school at all. Obviously, this was unrealistic. And did it really matter? It mattered to me, but did it matter to her? And would it be something that impacted the rest of her life? I thought not.

She kept her part-time job for the entire time she was in high school. It actually gave her some fairly good experience as she stayed at the same job for four years. It taught her how to be responsible and it taught her a good work ethic; both of which helped in her later endeavours.

Social Butterflies

When I was in school, I kept to myself. I didn't make friends easily. Because I focused on my school work and volunteer/paid work, I had great marks and I could get recommendations from any teacher, supervisor, or boss.

I didn't talk unless spoken to. Every time I voiced an opinion, the butterflies in my stomach dashed around madly trying to escape. I hated the feeling, so I barely talked. It wasn't until after university when I joined Toastmasters that I really began to make these butterflies fly in formation. But that's a topic for another book.

This trait was not, thankfully, passed on to my children. My daughter, in particular, is much more of a social butterfly than I am. While in school she made friends very easily. She wanted to hang out with her friends all the time. That may have been because she was the only child in our house until she was 14. I often used to joke that I saw her less often than her friends did. Ironically, it was the truth sometimes.

We did have to make a rule that she was home for supper at least five times per week while she was in school. Just so I could catch up and see what was going on in her life. This small act made our family stronger.

Even now that she is done school and working full time, she stops by a couple times a week just to say hi and visit for an hour or so. I love these visits. It's our time to catch up. Sometimes I think she only does it for me, but I know she has developed a strong bond with her brothers.

Do not discourage your kids from being social butterflies. It's one of the best traits they could have in the world—the ability to communicate and get along with others.

Sexual Preferences

My daughter's first real boyfriend was in Grade 8—the son of one of her favourite teachers. I had a hard time coming to grasp with her dating so young but that was my issue, not hers. That relationship lasted about a year. In high school, she started dating another boy.

The day I finally got to meet her second boyfriend, B pulled me aside and told me not to drill him about his mom's relationship. I looked at her quizzically and asked her to elaborate. She told me he had two moms. I think she expected me to be shocked or horrified. I took this opportunity to explain families come in all shapes and sizes. Some have married parents, some divorced, some have gay or lesbian parents, some have kids, and some have blended families. The point was—they loved each other.

I also explained I knew a lot of people who were trans, gay, lesbian, bisexual, and all variations. I told her there was nothing wrong with their lifestyles. I know her dad did not feel the same way—he was very homophobic.

I never did end up "drilling" the boyfriend about his parents. I wouldn't do that to any of her friends. Frankly, it's not my business. And it doesn't bother me. Everyone needs to be more tolerant of differences in the world.

Young Adults

My daughter, who was 20 at the time, came to me one day to say she and her boyfriend were moving in together into a townhouse. I was ecstatic. We eagerly chatted about her new place and how she was going to furnish it. Afterwards, she admitted to me she was hesitant to tell me because of the initial reaction from her boyfriend's parents. They were shocked when their son mentioned it to them as they had no prior heads up. At first, it seemed they were not too supportive. Thankfully, the shock soon passed.

It is such a shame when parents do not respect their children's choices. Especially when they are young adults. I had a very hard time earlier on, reminding myself that even if I didn't agree with a choice, it was not mine to make. I could provide information or opinion but, in the end, B was a grown up. I really had no say. I appreciated her listening to me. I tried not to be overly judgmental (though sometimes it was extremely difficult).

Once she was done high school and pursuing her first year of welding, she informed me she wanted to work in the oil and gas industry (before it crashed in 2015). She wanted to know if I would be disappointed in her because of my environmentalist views. I looked at her, paused, and said I would support her choices always, even if I did not agree with them. I didn't overreact. I didn't say how horrible it was for the environment or how sexist the oil rigs could be.

A few days later, she confided in me that a close friend had told her about the sexism in the industry. I breathed a silent sigh of relief as I nodded and shared the information I knew. I was glad she heard it from someone else first. I didn't want to be negative about her choices.

In the end, she did not go into oil and gas (or not yet anyway). She didn't even take work at the refinery within the city. She continued to work making bale movers at a small, independent retailer just outside the city.

Then came the purchase of the new house. Everyone was so happy for the couple. Then her biological dad said, "I guess I won't be visiting you." That took some of the water from her bucket, but she shrugged it off as best she could.

Your kids need your support. Always. No matter what. You can't fix their issues regardless of how hard you try. You can be there to support them, to catch them when they fall, to wipe their tears when they cry. You can hug them (every day or as often as they will let you). You can love them unconditionally and deal with the fallout as it comes. They are only human—just like you. And no one is perfect. No one.

Easter Egg Hunts

Easter egg hunts have always been a tradition in our house. We have learned many valuable lessons about how to hold a successful Easter egg hunt and how to maximize enjoyment—for the kids and the parents.

The first lesson we learned with hiding those little foil eggs is dogs will eat the eggs when you are not watching. Keep pets (especially dogs) away from the hidden goodies.

The second lesson we learned is Mom (or Dad) needs to remember where she (or he) hid them all. Throughout one year, I found eggs around the house that my kids hadn't found.

Next lesson: don't eat the eggs you find later in the year, they do go stale. (Yuck!)

Using the three lessons above, we found securing the animals in a room before starting the hunt and making a map of some sort would result in the most enjoyable experience for all. We even evolved the hunts as the children grew.

Our map started fairly simply—a page with pictures on it, like a treasure map. Even though I do not have mad drawing skills, the kids were always able to decipher the pictures. An example map might look like this:

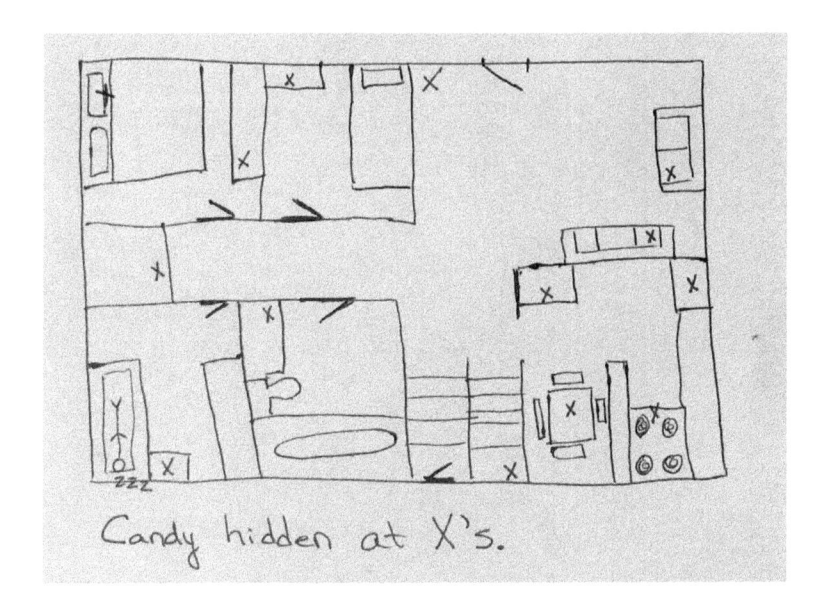

Candy hidden at X's.

Then we started doing more of a hunt without a map but with clues that led you from one candy stash to another. At first, these clues were pictures (when the children did not read yet). The hunt would start out with the picture of something simple like a couch:

The child would know to go to the table to find the chocolate and another picture:

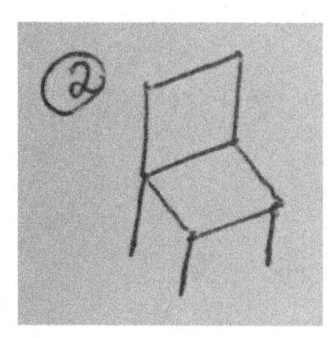

Then they would go to a chair. And so on:

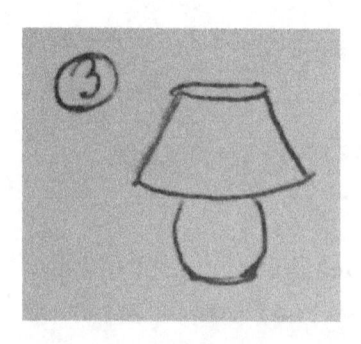

Things I Handled Like a Rock Star!

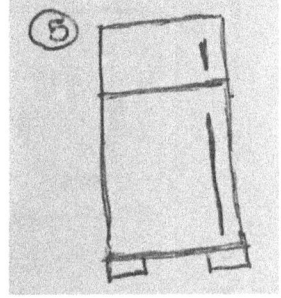

④

⑤

⑥

⑦

Following all the pictures would result in a big payoff with a large stash of candy and a stuffed animal. I liked to end the hunt with an item that allowed ample room—like the dryer or the oven:

Over the years the pictures became more complicated; for example, the picture of a lamp would be more challenging as there were multiple lamps in the house. (I know I used a lamp in the example above. In that case, it should be clear to a younger child which lamp you are referencing—for example, by walking with them to the lamp.)

When this type of search was getting too easy (usually once the child could read), we started using hints or riddles instead of pictures. An example might be: "You turn this on in the living room to see." The answer was "a lamp." Again, one clue would lead to the next until you found the large candy stash at the end.

These types of hunts with maps, pictures, or hints/riddles helped add fun to our Easter egg hunts (and we weren't finding eggs all over the house for months afterwards).

Christmas Presents Spy Game

D loves all things spy-related. There was a mail-out subscription we got him that involved learning how to be a spy. It had a book about spies and each shipment contained some new thing D needed to learn. He learned about cryptography and how different codes can be used to hide a message. He learned about traps and how to get around them. He became rather proficient at getting through the assignments that were sent.

It logically followed that D decided he wanted a spy game to get to the Christmas tree and presents one year. This variation on the Easter egg hunt included things he had learned in his spy "course" like cryptography puzzles, math problems, and booby traps.

My late husband got extremely creative with this request. He gave D a time limit of one hour to complete the challenge. J set up a "laser" trap D had to deactivate before he could get out of his bedroom. The lasers were just wool taped to the door frame on both sides, but D had to get through them (with scissors) without setting off the popsicle stick traps that were scattered around his room. The next challenge was finding the "code" (cryptography legend) to crack the secret message for the next stage. Completing a page of math questions provided the combination to the "safe" (a small cardboard box taped to the wall with numbers on it) where the cryptography legend was.

All that led our young spy downstairs to the dexterity challenge—D had to navigate through a "tunnel" (blanket) without bumping the sides. If the blanket moved or a bell (which hung inside the tunnel) rang, an "alarm" sounded, and D had to start again.

Eventually, D succeeded at making it through the challenge. How we will outdo this in future years, I do not know. (This chapter will self-destruct in three minutes.)

Picky Eaters

With my liver experience as a child, I refuse to force my kids to eat food they do not want to eat. That being said, I spend a lot of time and energy on meals. A nutritious, well-rounded meal takes at least 30 minutes to cook. Add prep and cleanup and I'm looking at spending at least an hour on a meal. I'm not going to make separate meals for the kids just because they don't like something in it.

B's choice of pickiness was chick peas in the chili. I would have her pick them out. Then I got vetoed once D was in the picture because *I* was the only one who liked them. So, *I* had to add them to *my* meal. B has since moved out and T likes them, so now D has to pick them out.

I have one boy (T) who likes tomatoes but not green peppers and another one (D) who likes green peppers but not tomatoes. Fajita night is always fun. LOL!

Meal prep, cooking and cleanup takes much too much time to make different meals for picky eaters. My house is not a restaurant (though some days I wish it was, so I didn't have to cook). If you don't like something in a meal, just pick it out. Or give it a try, you might even like it. D never used to want green beans but since he has tried them a few times, he now likes them.

Happy munching!

Gender Norms

Gender norms, for the purpose of this book, are defined as roles or traits that we, as a society, delegate as "normal" for a gender. As I already indicated in the introduction, I struggle with the definition of normal. Maybe a better definition would be roles or traits that a society or a generation consider acceptable for a traditional gender (i.e. male or female). Whether I agree with them or not, Canadian society dictates certain things and even if I do not impose these norms on my children, others do.

Career Choices

As a woman in a non-traditional role (Information Technology), I see people's career choices as something personal; something each person should be able to choose regardless of what others think. My daughter, for example, is a welder. She is in even more of a non-traditional role than I am. At least in my industry, the ratio of male to female is equalizing; however, with B, she was the *only* female in her third-year studies.

Her very first job as a welder ended fairly quickly—her choice. Not only was her employer violating labour laws, they made blatantly sexist comments to her.

B had her wisdom teeth surgically extracted shortly after she was employed. She notified her employer of this when she was hired as it was two weeks after her job started. Her dentist put her on "light duty" and provided a note to her employer.

She was on codeine. I know codeine in any amount usually puts *me* on my ass and I'm double her weight; I know better than to leave the house when I've taken it. Instead, B reported for duty. The employer's "light duty" still consisted of operating a grinder—a hand held machine that rotates an abrasive disk removing metal and paint from a surface. It rotates extremely fast and if it touches any part of your body, it will rip your skin. (My ex had it happen once.) Operating a grinder while on codeine is a significant health and safety risk!

When she explained this "light duty" work to me, I responded, "Um, no. You have the right to refuse unsafe work and this is unsafe work." I advised her to say exactly that to her boss. Her employer's response? "Don't take your pain medication." Um, *no*! At this point, her boss said something along the line of, "as a woman in welding, you're going to have to learn how to suck it up," referring to the pain. Um … NO!

She ended up taking the remainder of the week off to think about whether she wanted to continue her employment with them. She chose not to. And within a couple weeks, she had new employment at a superb shop where she worked for the next three years.

My recommendations to you as a parent if you are facing a gender norm crisis when it comes to the roles your children take on is to talk to them. Address your own bias, address society's bias, and encourage them to do what *they* think is right for themselves.

Pink Strollers

When D was very young (two or three), we would walk from home to the daycare in the morning. D was in a nurturing phase and had taken to pushing around a plush toy in his toy stroller. I had no issue with it at all. In fact, I went out and purchased the stroller for him.

One of my co-workers saw D pushing the stroller with his stuffy. Thankfully, she waited until after D was at daycare to comment on the complete faux pas I had committed with my child. She questioned, "Did the stroller have to be pink?"

As I explained that all the strollers I could find were pink, I thought to myself, what a ridiculous argument. Her issue wasn't with D pushing his stuffy around in a stroller (at least society has come far enough to accept males wanting to take part in parenting roles). It was the fact the stroller was pink.

I wish I had a better response to her inquiry at the time. One that was a little more philosophical and dove into why she didn't think a boy could pull off pink. "Tough guys wear pink," was the motto one year for the Calgary Stampede.

Nail Polish

Being a bit of a homophobe, my ex has an issue with D wearing nail polish. Even blue or orange. Little kids like to mimic what they see their parents doing, so when I was painting my nails, D would often ask to have his done. T does the same thing. I never saw the harm. Nail polish can be easily removed.

Yet, if I sent D over to visit his dad (who lived in the basement of Nana's house), both of them would natter at D about it. Eventually, D would ask me to remove it before he went over. I respected his wishes and did so even though I did not agree.

My co-worker's late husband, M, worked at the refinery so his nails would not come clean. His solution? Paint his nails. Granted it was usually black, but I used M as an example to prove males can (and do) wear nail polish.

As I previously mentioned, T likes to have his nails painted as well. His dad, my late husband, never let it bother him; as long as T was happy. I did make sure, again, the nail polish was a "boy" colour. Gramma doesn't necessarily agree with it; that may be a generational thing because lots of older people have this same belief.

Unfortunately, society dictates boys don't wear nail polish (for now anyway). Boys have to be tough; they can't be girly. Uh huh. What-ever (sashaying hand).

Girls Can't Be Truck Drivers

Proving someone wrong feels good. Admit it!

D matter-of-factly stated one day, "Girls can't be truck drivers."

When I questioned this, his reasoning was, "Daddy said so."

No matter how I tried to explain it, it was not until a few weeks later when he saw a female driving a semi-truck that he believed me.

In fact, now he has a special female trucker friend, R, who his Gramma introduced him to. He got to sit in the semi-truck and took home a few souvenirs!

Girls (and boys) can be anything they want to be!

The Path to Perfection

Paddling Pools

When my first child was young, we lived in Saskatoon, which is about a three-hour drive from Regina where we currently live. The city used to have a supervised paddling pool across the street from us. It was nice because although the water was refilled daily, by the time it was afternoon, it was lukewarm and enjoyable. We spent a lot of time there over the course of seven summers while I finished university. It was a shallow pool—maybe a foot-deep maximum. But it was free, and it was fun.

We moved to Regina when B was nine. The first thing we noticed was there were no paddling pools; instead there were spray pads. For those of you who have not had the pleasure (can you say oxymoron?) of a spray pad, let me try to explain it to you. Spray pads usually have a concrete base with various connections and contraptions that spray icy cold water out of them. And when I say icy, I mean icy; they don't warm up throughout the day. The other day, T was shivering so badly, his teeth were chattering. Despite this, he would not leave. Pleasurable is *not* the word I would use when describing spray pads. Like most parents, I try to stay out of the direct spray—getting only my feet wet or staying far enough away so only mist hits me.

There were also two free city pools: one in North Central ("The Hood") and one in Heritage ("The Hood Lite")—two of the sketchiest areas of town. Because these two pools do not meet the current codes, they are free. They are also supervised. However, the shallowest end is over three-feet deep, so any small child needs to be held or put in a floatation device. Every summer, these pools are packed full because they are in socioeconomically challenged areas of town and they are free.

The City of Regina keeps trying to close them, but the Heritage Community Association and residents always fights them to keep their pool (Maple Leaf) open. In 2018, the city (amid massive public pressure) finally agreed to rebuild Maple Leaf pool. However, nothing was said about the one in North Central—it will probably be replaced with a spray pad.

If I had my preference, I would choose shallow paddling pools over both the spray pads and the free city pools. I know, I should not complain. At least we have a (free) option to cool down in over the summer time. First world problem, I know.

Help Me Fix My Car

My daughter was in Grade 8 when we bought our first house. It was in a different school zone, but she wanted to keep going to the school where she had started that year, so we bought her a bus pass and let her take the bus to and from school. The public city bus B took resulted in her having to walk part-way home (about eight blocks).

Normally, this would not have been an issue. However, we had bought a house in a neighbourhood I refer to as "The Hood Lite." While it does not have as much crime as North Central Regina, it is a close second. On a map of Regina the city police have on their website, our house is directly under the huge red dot representing criminal activities. One of my acquaintances told me the city police consider North Central the jelly in the jelly donut; you don't squeeze it because it will ooze out into the rest of the city. A nice euphemism eh?

Anyway, my then twelve-year-old daughter had enough knowledge (imparted by an over protective parent) and street savvy to know how to handle most situations. Such as the time one guy asked her to help him fix his car. She looked at him like he was crazy, said no, and kept walking. Seriously?!? Like a twelve-year-old is going to know anything about how to fix a car.

When she got home and relayed this to me, we had a little laugh. I told her she should just start twitching and muttering loudly to herself. If someone asked her what she was saying, to respond, "I wasn't talking to you." We had a good laugh as we brainstormed more realistic ideas of how to handle this sort of (silly) request in the future.

Making Songs Out of Anything

Kids love music. (Doesn't everyone?) My youngest child *loves* it when I make up new lyrics to existing songs. They don't even have to make sense, as long as they are to some type of rhythm. And if the song has actions, even better.

Over the years, we have come up with a semi-exhaustive list of every possible function of a bus. You can also substitute car, truck, train, plane, etc. for bus. Actions are optional but included for your pleasure.

Wheels on the Bus (Semi-exhaustive version)

1. **Verse:** The wheels on the bus go round and round, round and round, round and round. The wheels on the bus go round and round, all through the town.

   Action: Put your arms horizontally in front of you, with elbows bent (so they are in front of your chest and one arm is overlapping the other). Rotate your arms around each other mimicking wheels turning.

2. **Verse:** The doors on the bus go open and shut, open and shut, open and shut. The doors on the bus go open and shut, all through the town.

   Action: Clap your hands together gently and pull apart. Repeat.

3. **Verse:** The driver on the bus says, "move on back, move on back, move on back." The driver on the bus says, "move on back" all through the town.

Action: Close your fist with your thumb sticking out. Motion with your thumb over your shoulder repeatedly to move on back.

4. **Verse:** The change on the bus goes "chink, chink, chink"...

   Action: Mimic dropping change into the change slot.

5. **Verse:** The pass on the bus goes "bing, bing, bing"...

   Action: Mimic swiping a card over a reader.

6. **Verse:** The people on the bus go up and down...

   Action: Straighten your back all the way and then scrunch down. Or move your arm up and down.

7. **Verse:** The babies on the bus go, "wah, wah, wah"...

   Action: Pretend to rub your eyes with your fist.

8. **Verse:** The mommies on the bus go, "shh, shh, shh" ...

   Action: Put your pointer finger over your lips as you say, "Shh shh shh."

9. **Verse:** The daddies on the bus go, "I love you"...

   Action: Point at your eye on "I"; your heart on "love"; your child on "you."

10. **Verse:** The grammas on the bus go gossip, gossip, gossip...

    Action: Pretend you are holding a puppet on your hand and you are making it talk with your fingers.

11. **Verse:** The grampas on the bus go, "hmph, hmph, hmph"...

    Action: Make a grumpy face as you say each "hmph."

12. **Verse:** The teens on the bus go click, click, send...

    Action: Pretend you are texting on a phone.

13. **Verse:** The phones on the bus go, "ring, ring, ring"...

    Action: Form a pretend phone with your hand—your pinky is the place you speak into by your mouth, your thumb hovers by your ear so you can hear, your other 3 fingers are bent (to keep them out of the way).

14. **Verse:** The lights on the bus go on and off...

    Action: Put your hands in front of your chest, palms out. Splay your fingers out and then close them into a fist—repeatedly.

15. **Verse:** The engine on the bus goes, "vroom, vroom, vroom"...

    Action: Mimic switching gears on a motorcycle with your hands (revving the engine).

16. **Verse:** The wipers on the bus go swish, swish, swish...

    Action: Put your arms in front of you, with elbows bent (so both hands are pointing straight up from the elbows). Swish your arms left and right like wipers cleaning the windshield.

17. **Verse:** The toilets on the bus go flush, flush, flush...

    Action: Pretend you are flushing a toilet (pressing the lever or button). (Yes, I know most public transit busses don't have toilets, but the long-distance ones do.)

18. **Verse:** The wheel on the bus goes, "hiiisssssss"...

    Action: None. (Tire is going flat slowly.)

19. **Verse:** The mechanic on the bus goes, "don't worry"...

    Action: Shake your head.

20. **Verse:** The people on the bus have found a spare...

    Action: Point like you've found something.

21. **Verse:** The mechanic on the bus goes, "jack it up"...

    Action: Pretend you are pressing on the handle of a jack.

22. **Verse:** The wheels on the bus go round again ...

    Action: See the first verse.

23. **Verse:** The kids on the bus go, "mind my feet"...

    Action: Point at your foot.

24. **Verse:** The gas on the bus goes, "glug, glug, glug" ...

    Action: Mimic drinking from a cup.

25. **Verse:** The radio on the bus goes, "tra la la" ...

    Action: Wiggle fingers in the air.

26. **Verse:** The windows on the bus go up and down...

    Action: Use your arm—point up then down. Repeat.

Okay, I'm sure this is *not* an exhaustive list—you can probably think of many more examples. But *I'm* exhausted so that's it for me.

Make up Lyrics

If you have an instrumental song like Brahm's Lullaby, you can make up words to it:

"Go to sleep, little man, close your big beautiful eyes, I know you're tired little man, so close your eyes and go to sleep."

T loves this one—with the music playing softly in the background.

Change up Lyrics

Changing up lyrics to an existing song is not difficult; it just requires a bit of creativity. You will have to ensure the syllable count of the original song remains for the lyrics to be effective.

"One Little Finger" can be changed to "One Little Paw-Paw." (Referring to Paw Patrol—one of T's favourite shows.)

One little paw paw
One little paw paw
One little paw paw, tap tap tap
Point your paw up, point your paw down
Put it on your [head, nose, chin, arm, legs]

Take the song "Five Little Monkeys" (jumping on the bed) and change it to the animal of your choice—duckies, rabbits, kitties, etc.

Five little duckies jumping on the bed
One fell off and bumped his head
Mama called the doctor
And the doctor said, "No more duckies jumping on the bed."

Four little rabbits jumping on the bed
One fell off and bumped his head
Mama called the doctor
And the doctor said, "No more rabbits jumping on the bed."

Three little kitties jumping on the bed
One fell off and bumped her head
Mama called the doctor
And the doctor said, "No more kitties jumping on the bed."

Two little doggies jumping on the bed
One fell off and bumped his head

Mama called the doctor
And the doctor said, "No more doggies jumping on the bed."

One little <child's name> jumping on the bed
S/he fell off and bumped her/his head
Mama called the doctor
And the doctor said, "Put that <child's name> right to bed."

Another example is taking "One Elephant Went Out to Play Upon a Spider Web One Day" and changing it to "One Little Duck (friend, cat, dog—whatever your child's favourite animal is) Went Out to Play Upon a Splashy Pond One Day":

One little duck went out to play
Upon a splashy pond one day
He had such enormous fun
That he called for another little duck to come.

Then switch up the animals and/or places if you want:

Two little cats went out to play
With a scratching post one day
They had such enormous fun
That they called for another little cat to come.

Three little dogs went out to play
At the doggie park one day
They had such enormous fun
That they called for another little dog to come.

Four little mice went out to play
Inside a big red barn one day
They had such enormous fun
That they called for another little mouse to come.

Five little friends went out to play
Upon a splashy pond one day
They had such enormous fun
They forgot to go home when they were done.

The possibilities are endless. Have fun with this. Laugh and giggle. Match your child's interest with the song—favourite show, favourite animal, or favourite activity. And sing away. Don't stress about what you sound like. Only your child is listening and (hopefully) joining you.

Rock a Bye Baby

This is a popular nursery rhyme we sing in Canada (and likely other countries):

Rock a bye baby on the tree top, when the wind blows, the cradle will rock. When the bough breaks, the baby will fall. Down will come baby, cradle and all.

I find these lyrics to be kind of morbid (I mean, who talks about having a baby falling out of the tree?) so I modified it when I sang to my children:

Rock a bye baby on the tree top, when the wind blows, the cradle will rock. When the bough sways, the baby will sleep; all through the night o-oh so deep.

I found this version a little more appealing, though it still left me questioning who would put their baby in a tree. But we can't all be perfect, can we?

Dance Like No One is Watching

Not only do kids love music, they also love dancing! Setting up a dance party in the living room is a lot of fun—not only can the adults get in some exercise, it tuckers the kids out. We put YouTube on the (smart) TV and alternate between picking songs. Then we let our creative dance moves shine. Sometimes we dance with scarves. Sometimes other items. Sometimes in our underwear. Whatever we feel like. My youngest likes the "kitty dance" where he's down on all fours like a kitty and wiggling around, whereas D likes to "floss" his butt.

My youngest has been known to "bust a move" in stores when a good song comes on. He just stops and starts bobbing his head and moving his body. It makes me smile every time he does it. Sometimes I even join in.

Walking to work is much more fun with music on. It makes the time go faster. I often walk in time to the music and bebop to the beat while waiting for the walk light. I may look ridiculous, but life is too short not to dance. So, dance like no one is watching—they are probably too busy staring at their phones anyway.

Grocery Shopping

Do you hate shopping at a certain big box grocery store that starts with "S?" I feel like a cow being herded through a cattle gate as I unload the groceries in my cart onto the "to pay" conveyer belt, tell the cashier I don't need any bags, and start to pack up my groceries. Meanwhile the cashier is pushing her button control that moves the "rung in" groceries further and further down another conveyer belt (squashing all the items in the meantime), I despise shopping here but the prices cannot be beat and so I drag my butt (and my children) there each month to shop for groceries. Sometimes even more often, as I hate the big box store that starts with "W" even more.

When my late husband was sick, I often had to take both boys grocery shopping. Some days it could be extremely difficult to round up both my helpers. On this particular day, things were going exceptionally well.

As I was nearly finished packing up my groceries, a middle-aged woman put her hand on my arm and simply said, "I just have to say, you are an awesome mom." I beamed at her and replied, "Thank you." With smiles on both our faces, she turned to leave, and I finished packing.

She has no idea how much that meant to me to have a complete stranger realize how hard it was to maintain my stress level (and my temper) while keeping my two boys (age two and eight at the time) entertained with "helping" as I was herded through the checkout lane. Moooo!

Can I Have a Bunny?

When she was younger, my daughter would sometimes see wild rabbits in the city. Not nearly as often as we do now, but from time to time one would hop into our line of view.

Like most children, whenever a cute, furry animal was around the questions of, "Can I have a <insert animal here>?" would arise. The answer for a lot of parents is an automatic, "No."

Regardless of the reasoning I gave—like how much work pets were or how much they cost, B would do one or more of the following: become crestfallen, sullen and/or withdrawn; pout or whine; cry; or reason.

As I mentioned in the chapter entitled "Saying No," one of my parental goals was to reduce the number of times I gave "no" as an answer. Some quote I read said that children heard the word "no" about 15,000 times more often than they heard "yes." We pass on negativity 15,000 times more often than we pass on positivity. That's kind of scary, don't you think?

My solution? "If you can catch the bunny, you can keep it." Brash? Daring? Risk-taking? Indubitably. If she did manage to catch one, we would have to keep our promise to adopt it. It was definitely risky, but it made her smile at the prospect of having a bunny. If she could catch one.

Then it became a game of bunny chasing. I would encourage her to (safely) catch any rabbit she saw. She tried chasing; she tried coaxing with food; she tried calling it like she called a cat, "here bunny bunny." Yeah, she got frustrated from time to time but she persevered in trying to catch one—for over a year.

Thankfully though, she never did catch one and we never had to adopt a bunny.

Hop

When my youngest boy started daycare around age 18 months, the center was near Pioneer Village (a senior's independent housing facility). There was a large, open, grassy area right across the street. Residents liked to leave nibblies outside for the local wildlife and as a result, there was often at least one rabbit hopping around the area.

My son named all bunnies (stuffed or real) Hop (because that's what bunnies do). I mean it makes sense, doesn't it? With his limited vocabulary, he could communicate in a clear manner using single words. He liked to chase Hop around the field. When my late husband was feeling okay, they would spend a good hour frolicking in the grassy area as T squealed in delight and ran after the rabbit. It appeared almost every day. We would look for Hop when we dropped T off and J and T would chase him after daycare.

I got to witness it one day on a day off from work. It was the cutest, most exhausting game ever. Funny thing, the bunny never left the open field—he just went around and around, stopping from time to time to let T catch up. And it kept coming back day after day, week after week. I couldn't really keep up with T but as it was an open field, I couldn't lose sight of him and the duo always ended up coming back my way (repeatedly).

When I have a stressful day, I no longer have to "stop to smell the flowers"—I can now stop to watch T chase Hop. Such a simple thing brought joy to so many family members.

Calgary Bus Trip

B must have been about five or six when we planned our first road trip to Calgary. At the time, I was in university and my ex-husband was working full time (though our income was only about $1700/month pre-tax). This resulted in us having a not-so-reliable car—one that I would not have chanced taking on the highway—so we chose to take the bus (Greyhound/STC). Plus, it was cheaper to take the bus—even with three of us.

We anticipated a fabulous trip. Excitement buzzed around the household. One of my hubby's friends was going to put us up so we didn't have to pay for a hotel which was awesome because we were on a budget.

We chose to book a late bus; leaving at 10 p.m. Our theory was we could sleep on the bus. There were a couple of flaws in that theory.

First, B announced happily, "I'm going to stay awake the *whole* ride!"

Um, that threw a wrench in our plans if she actually did. Smiling, we agreed she could stay awake as long as she wanted. We figured she'd last maybe an hour. We didn't even make it to the edge of Saskatoon and she was fast asleep.

Second flaw. Have you ever tried to sleep on a bus? It's worse than sleeping sitting up in a car. At least in a car, you can tilt the seat back and use a pillow or jacket to lean against the door. In a bus, even if you have a window seat, there is no possible way to get comfortable. If you are unfortunate enough to have an aisle seat, you have nowhere to lean. Thankfully, the bus wasn't completely full so B, being so small, could stretch out across two seats. My ex hubby and I didn't rest much between being uncomfortable, general noise on the bus, and stops every hour or so.

About halfway there, we made a stop in Hanna, Alberta (birthplace of the soon-to-be-popular band, Nickelback) where there was an aquarium with *huge* fish swimming in it. The teeth on these fish were enormous. After a short washroom break, we were back on the bus to finish the ride to Calgary.

As we had never been to Calgary before as a family, there was lots to see and do. The folks we stayed with showed us around a bit. We caught the late bus home and B didn't manage to stay awake on the way back either.

Bribing with Broccoli

B always loved vegetables. She would eat them over meat anytime. And she *loved* broccoli. I mean *loved* the stuff. I never had to bribe her to eat it. She would inhale it quicker than candy when I served it.

On one of my first dates with my ex-husband in Saskatoon we went to supper at a Chinese buffet. B was around age two. She was fussing at eating what was left on her plate and so I told her, "You can have more broccoli if you finish eating what's on your plate."

My ex looked up at me, watching in shock as B gobbled up what was left on her plate and I rewarded her with her coveted vegetable. He muttered something like, "That really works with her?"

I never thought any differently; it was instinct as a parent to bribe my child. It never occurred to me at the time that I was bribing her with something healthy. It worked for me. And to this day, B isn't a sugar-a-holic like I am. She likes to eat healthy food over junk.

Ironically, both my boys like broccoli as well, although I haven't bribed them with it to finish what's on their plate. Not yet, anyway.

PART 3

Pearls of Wisdom

*L*ife is what happens while you're making other plans. Sometimes we make plans about how we are going to raise our children based on the past journeys we have experienced. Then the reality of life hits. My late spouse and I intended to bring our last child up together; to teach him based on our past parenting experience. Then cancer took my spouse and I found myself a single mom of two young boys (my oldest had moved out years prior). I learned a lot about present moment mindfulness during my spouse's diagnosis, treatment, and eventual death. It's not life after death that matters, it's the living before death that is critical.

Pull out your Kleenex for this next part of the trip—it's full of ups and downs and the weather is stormy with periods of sunshine (or vice versa).

Underage Drinking

When my daughter turned 16, she asked if she could have a drink during her birthday party. I told her she could have up to five as long as she wasn't driving anywhere.

The day after her birthday, I met her at the mall for lunch. She brought her best friend and her boyfriend. She was looking a little rough. I asked her how her night was. She indicated she only had five drinks. I asked her, "Did you puke?"

Her boyfriend burst out laughing. It was not the question he expected. He was anticipating I would be mad. Maybe that's what his mom would have done.

My daughter sheepishly answered, "Yes."

I laughed and said, "Good."

Her boyfriend laughed again as he heard another answer he did not expect.

I thought it was interesting that she drank so little and had gotten sick. But she was a new drinker, so it wasn't really unreasonable. Throughout the lunch we talked about her party.

During the conversation I deduced her one "drink" was a three ounce one. Now I had specified five drinks; I had not specified one ounce per drink. Technically, she had followed the rules, but that explained why she became ill.

I tell you she didn't drink again until her trip to Cuba when she was 18. And when she did drink again, it was in moderation. Sometimes life experience is the best learning tool.

Marijuana

Unlike my willingness to allow my child to experiment with alcohol, experimenting with drugs was not something I smiled upon.

My ex-husband liked to smoke marijuana. A lot. In fact, that is part of the reason why our marriage ended. It was a constant thorn in my side though I don't know if it was the drug per se as we were together for 15 years and I was aware he smoked it well before I married him. More likely it was the lifestyle he was leading in general. Like he had his own little world I was no longer part of.

There were a couple of instances in our marriage that our daughter saw my ex's bong. (A bong is a glass contraption you fill part way with water and smoke marijuana through.) He was usually fairly good with making sure it was put away, but not always. And once, my daughter (in her early teenage years) found it on the shelf by our back door and asked what it was. I didn't know what to say other than, "It's your Dad's." (Avoidance.)

Unfortunately, my daughter and her boyfriend did start experimenting with marijuana. I guess I found it ironic though when my ex-husband decided to lecture her about it her usage. I didn't know whether to laugh or cry.

Again, it comes down to trusting our children even if we don't agree with their choices. If it was a more extreme drug, I might've planned an intervention. Now it's legal here in

Canada, so it will become even more prevalent than it was. I need to get with the times man. LOL!

Pain

My late husband often suffered from various aches and pains. As a very active person and personal trainer, he had joint issues.

We tried various remedies to help ease his pain—painkillers, ice, rubs, Reiki, massage, and acupuncture were some of the pain management techniques we undertook.

My middle boy was four when he simply stated to J one day, "I want to punch the pain." It was the sweetest thing the way he said it. As if he could just take it away from J by punching it.

Friend Versus Parent

People have told me, when you are a parent, you should not be a "friend" to your child. I don't know if I agree with this statement.

According to the Oxford Dictionary, "Friendship is a relationship of mutual affection between two or more people." Is a parent-child relationship not, by this definition, a friendship then?

As parents, we should, no doubt, be the guiding force or leader for our child(ren). However, to not be their friend is an oxymoron.

Most of us guide our children through love—what is best for them. We make rules to keep them safe, not just rules for the sake of rules. Rules like "don't play on the road" just make sense coming from a parent to a child. Yet a friend would say that, too. (I hope.)

Your parent-child relationship evolves as your child becomes an adult. I became more of a friend and confidant to my daughter as she entered adulthood. We could talk about anything. I knew not to burden her with too many of my problems, but I let her know I was there to talk about anything with her: birth control, boys, sex, spats with girlfriends, buying a house, problems at work, dealing with people, drinking, drugs, tattoos, and so on. No topic was off-limits. Granted, the topic was adjusted to the age of the audience at the time, but it was never shrugged off (except the bong incident a couple chapters back).

My solution? Be the parent but be the friend, too. Know where to draw the line.

Needles

Twenty years ago, I had to teach my daughter not to pick up needles buried in the sand at the playground. Sad, I know. But a necessary evil because we lived in a rough area of town and there were a lot of times we found discarded needles in the sand.

Fast forward to today and I had to teach my middle child not to pick them up in our neighbourhood. Thankfully, we have not found any in the playground.

It is likely I will have to teach my youngest son this as well.

The irony in this came when my middle child got upset at me for picking up a discarded needle off the ground to dispose of it properly. Once I had explained to him I was using safety precautions and I would ensure another child did not pick it up, he was okay with it.

The happy part is, he listened to me about it. He heard what I said and attempted to get me to follow my own teachings.

Dealing with Violence

My late husband and I were discussing one of the school shootings in the United States while driving in the car one day. D was in the backseat; he was three or four.

As Canadians, many of us don't understand what would possess someone to walk into a school (especially an elementary school) and start shooting at children. On second thought, as *human beings*, many of us don't understand this. It's not just Canadians—I'm sure people across the globe asked themselves, "What the hell?"

It remains unclear to me why these massacres continue to happen within the borders of our southern neighbor. In "Bowling for Columbine," Michael Moore wondered the same thing. He proposed several theories including that guns and ammunition are too easily accessible in the States, whereas in Canada, they aren't.

I don't recall what exactly J and I were saying about the incident. We thought we were talking quietly until I heard D say, "They should have used their words, Mom."

Indeed D, they should have used their words.

Sam and Dean

Laundromats suck. Let's be honest. If you've ever rented an apartment or had your washing machine break down, chances are you've had experience with laundromats. They are handy because you can (usually) get all your laundry done at the same time (versus waiting for a single machine in an apartment complex). However, nothing beats having your own machines in your residence. You can get your laundry done when *you* want to do it. And you don't have to spend hours fighting for use of the machines and waiting for the cycles to end. (You don't have to scrounge for change either.)

After purchasing our first house, my favourite room quickly became the laundry room. No, I'm not kidding. After renting for twenty-some odd years, having my own washer and dryer was exciting.

At our housewarming party, we decided to hold a contest to name the washer and dryer. A good friend of mine suggested

Sam and Dean (from Supernatural—our favourite show at the time). I loved it.

When I inquired as to which was Sam and which was Dean, my daughter (who was 14 at the time—and also loved the show) simply stated, "Sam's the washer and Dean's the dryer."

"Why?" I asked.

"Because Sam is cute, but Dean is hot," came the quick (and true) response.

After we stopped laughing at this brilliant deduction, we had a winner. I joked for a while after that night that Sam and Dean were definitely the hardest working men in the house. At least before I met J.

To Flu Shot or Not to Flu Shot

I have to admit, I sit on the fence on this topic. I believe, wholeheartedly, in immunizing my children when it comes to normal childhood vaccines. These vaccines have been tried, tested, and true in preventing these diseases. I'm talking diseases like measles, mumps, rubella and diptheria.

But when it comes to the flu shot, I'm torn. First, the flu mutates. Having a flu shot once or twice in your life is not sufficient. When a child is immunized against small pox, they have half a dozen shots and they are good. They won't catch that virus. Period. We've pretty much wiped out those diseases. Not so with the flu. The more we vaccinate against it, the more resilient the virus seems to become.

In talking to a healthcare worker at a vaccination booth one year, I learned that the powers-that-be high up in the medical community guess at which strain of the flu will circulate. Yes, they make a guess. I'm sure it's an educated one but it's a guess nonetheless. If they vaccinate for the wrong one, no one is protected.

When people do get sick and/or die, no one divulges which strain caused the illness versus which was vaccinated against that year. In fact, finding out if the person had *any* vaccine (not to mention the right one) is impossible due to privacy laws.

Second, I get sick after getting a flu shot. Almost every time. Sure, it's not as bad as it could be but it's still a bother. I've heard many others who say the same thing. But if children got a "mild" case of the mumps, small pox or rubella after their vaccinations, would anyone keep immunizing?

Third, okay, I'm digressing a bit into conspiracy theory here but seriously. If anyone wanted to wipe out a population, vaccines would be a quick way to do this. Oh, it's urgent, people have died from H1N1. Quick, get out there and get your flu shot. Then everyone goes and gets it and bam, everyone dies. Depopulation theory—Google it.

Fourth, flu vaccines come out after flu season starts. Wouldn't you want to be proactive? Have it out in July or August in preparation for December. Just saying.

Finally, and this is the kicker for me. Amidst the claims "People are dying! Quick, get out there and get your flu shot!" we hear:

- ∞ Oh, we've been swamped, we'll have to open more clinics.
- ∞ Oh wait, we've run out of vaccine (http://www.cbc.ca/news/canada/saskatchewan/regina-clinic-runs-out-of-flu-vaccine-1.2489077).
- ∞ According to http://www.cbc.ca/news/canada/saskatchewan/saskatchewan-starts-restricting-who-gets-flu-shots-1.2491842, they are now immunizing only those under five and pregnant women. Yet, of the seven who died in Saskatchewan in 2014, did *any* of them fall in this category? I believe, and I could be mistaken, the ones in Saskatchewan that year were in neither of these groups and all had underlying health issues. So, wouldn't it be better to restrict the vaccine to those with underlying health issues?

I just don't know. Personally, I'm leaning more towards not getting (flu) vaccinated. However, when it comes to my son (who is currently four), I should get one for him. *shaking my head*

Parenting Through Divorce

My daughter was 17 when I divorced my first husband. He wasn't her biological dad, but he had been her dad for most of her life. We met when she was one.

Through many conversations and a lot of tears, she and I came to work through our thoughts and feelings about the breakdown of our family unit. I tried to explain that it wasn't because I didn't love her dad anymore; it was because I couldn't live with him any longer. I tried not to speak ill of him in front of her. They continue to have a good relationship.

A counsellor helped my daughter explain her feelings to me. We had some open, honest communication about this. Even I needed a counsellor to work through my issues at the time.

There are hard times in everyone's lives. I guess the thing to do is just to work through them and cope the best you can. Get help from a professional as well, if required. I'm not ashamed to say I've seen counsellors too many times to count and I will continue to do so.

Divorced Versus Single Parenting

A fellow parent once commented to me there was an enormous difference between being a divorced parent and a single parent. I realized this was the truth.

As a divorced parent, you get a break from your child(ren), depending on your custody agreement. Your child(ren) are in the care of your ex and you get some much needed "you" time. With my first child this was a welcome reprieve, as my ex-husband and I could have a date night. With my second child, the visitations were (and continue to be) more sporadic. It was still a nice break when I had a weekend to myself once a month.

However, when my third child arrived (and my late spouse was still with us), we never really got a break (together) from having a child around the house. D would go to visit his dad, but T was still at home. I still got time to myself though, because J would watch T if I wanted to do something.

When J passed, I became a single parent. At the time of this writing, it has been exactly one year. I'm on my own now. I don't get a break; unless I hire a babysitter (which usually costs $10/hr) or Gramma or B watches the boys. I have a 24 hour, on-call job; 365 days a year for the next decade until my youngest can take care of himself for short periods.

It's exhausting really; physically, mentally and emotionally draining. I love my kids, please don't get me wrong. Sometimes though, I look forward to going to work after I've been at home for a weekend, alone with the boys.

As a single parent my kids get the best of me and the worst of me. They get the loving mom, but they also get the sad mom, the anxious mom, the angry mom, the playful mom, the exhausted mom, and the list goes on.

If you are divorced and you do manage to have some "you" time, please be sure to thank your ex-spouse (even if you don't really like him or her for any other reason).

School Marks

B got through elementary school with fairly decent marks. When she got to high school she became a lot more social and her marks dropped a little bit.

As an "A" student myself, it took some conscious effort for me to realize her marks would not be the same as mine. And it wasn't a bad thing because she was much more social than I was. She had a good group of friends to hang out with.

She worked a part-time job. And her marks were good; they just weren't A's.

There was some debate in the house about what classes she should take in high school. I wanted her to take all of the maths and sciences at the bare minimum. In Grade 10, she did this upon my request. Then before Grade 11 she told me she wanted to drop physics. I still encouraged her to take all of the sciences, but she was adamant she did not enjoy physics. (Truth be told, it was my least favourite of the sciences as well.) She would continue in all the maths and take chemistry and biology. It was a compromise. Again, I had to examine my motives. I wanted her to be able to make her own choices. And she was top of the class in some things like welding, which she really enjoyed (and later pursued as a career).

It's hard to let your child make (what you consider) life altering choices. But you know what? It is the duty of the parent to bring up their child the best they can and trust that their child can make their own decisions at some point. It's very hard to let this go for some people. But it's important to let your high school student follow their own path. The most important thing was she stayed in school.

As it turns out, she did very well for herself. She got a scholarship to go to SIAST and take welding. I was able to contribute towards her education, so she has no student loans to repay. Now she has a job as a welder and she's attained her journeyperson's certification. Things have turned out very well for her. I am proud of her and I respect her decisions, even if I don't agree with them.

With my second and third children, it remains to be seen how they do in school. So far, so good. My second one just finished Grade 3. He is one smart cookie and has my knack for math. T is not in school yet but he's smart too—he picks up a lot of things (some you wish he didn't).

Don't expect perfection from your child's school marks. In the end whether they get an A or a D, they learned something.

And they may have other skills that will turn out to be more important in life—like being social.

The Sanctity of Marriage

I have eight moms. I only have one biological mother and I am not adopted. So, how, you ask, do I have eight moms? Well, my dad has married eight times (and divorced seven times). Yes, you heard me right, eight times! At the time of writing this chapter, I had only recently found out my biological father was married for the 8th time to a woman slightly older than my age. This last one was a marriage of convenience (I believe) to get the woman immigrated to Canada but the other seven were legitimate marriages. And they were consecutive, not polygamist marriages. Which I guess would be a whole nother ball game.

I have half brothers and sisters I do not know at all. I don't know three of the women my dad married, either. I know of several, but I only keep in touch with two (my biological mom and my dad's 7th wife). Imagine if I knew all of these people; I would have a full Christmas list for mailing out letters!

Gone are the days when people got married once and stayed married to that person for their entire life. At the time of writing, my (now ex) husband and I were celebrating our 13th year of marriage. That isn't long and yet, so many people said, "wow" when I told them that. How many of you actually know couples that are still together after 10 years? 15? 20? 25?

When we were in our premarital class in Saskatoon in 1998, there were eight to ten couples in the class and the first thing we were told was to look around and realize over half of us would be divorced at some point in our lives. Seriously!?! A 50% chance of being divorced? Well, I guess when you consider my dad's divorce rate was 88% on his eight marriages ... it would take seven successful marriages to offset his record.

People getting married early doesn't happen that much anymore, either. If it does happen, it often doesn't last long. I knew a guy in university who had just turned 20, had a child, and was already divorced.

What happened to putting effort into relationships? All relationships are effort. Is it not worth someone's time and energy to work out the differences in a relationship that is already established rather than start all over with a new person? I know our marriage took a lot of effort. I can't tell you the number of times we went to a counsellor, but you know what? I'm not ashamed to tell people that.

Which brings me to the sanctity of marriage. There are religious zealots out there who condemn same-sex marriages because it defies the "sanctity of marriage." Seriously? *Seriously?* What about high divorce rates (50% of marriages ending in divorce)? Don't these impact marital sanctity? Or multiple marriages (seven ex-spouses) like my dad and Elizabeth Taylor (who I think has two up on my dad)? I can't count the number of celebrities who have caught their spouses cheating (according to the tabloids). And there is a website that enables people to have affairs with other married people (Ashleymadison.com). The website has 5.5 million users! And yet somehow, same sex marriages are going to wreck the sanctity of marriage!?!

Some people aren't even willing to get married anymore. So many people I know are common-law. They don't want that piece of paper to say it's legitimate in someone else's eyes. And I don't think that's necessarily wrong. You're not going to burn in hell, despite what the pastors and preachers tell you.

It seems to me the "sanctity" of marriage is no longer what it used to be between people not wanting to put effort in, divorce rates being so high, cheating being almost condoned by sites like AshleyMadison, and the increase of common-law marriages. I can vouch for this as I have eight moms because of my dad's marriages. The ironic thing is, Dad thinks the issue in the relationships were the women …

Contradicting Rules

It was, what I thought, an innocent Facebook post containing pictures of visibly upset children sitting on Santa's lap. My written comment was a question about why we force children to do this. Well, the shit storm it stirred up amongst my friends took me by surprise. The comments, both for and against, came instantaneously and flooded my notifications box.

Some people thought it was just funny to have their kids upset; the pictures were amusing (and yet sad).

Others attacked me outright stating that subjecting our kids to this type of experience was a rite of passage and that by not doing it, I was somehow doing a disservice to my child; I was coddling her.

Regardless of the responses I gave, those who were opposed remained so. I could not convince any of these folks to stop and think about this from a child's perspective.

There are some basic life lessons I was taught and (kind of) passed on to my children. Yet somehow, with reference to the Santa incident, we are teaching our children contradicting rules.

Stranger Danger

Let's define a stranger as anyone we don't know, for the purpose of this book.

Don't talk to strangers. It seems simple enough. I'm pretty sure any parent in any society has some variation of this rule. It's a safety thing; if a stranger tries to engage a child in conversation (usually without the parent in hearing distance), the child is not to answer.

It stands to reason from this rule, if you don't talk to strangers, you definitely don't leave with one. Again, it's a safety thing.

Yes, it could be fear-mongering but as parents, we don't want our children interacting with strangers who could potentially assault or abduct them.

Enter Santa Claus—a fictional figure who represents Christmas to many children across the world. The jolly bearded old man dressed in red on the television is just another animated figure—not a stranger. But a real, live person (almost exclusively male) dressed up in a Santa costume, sporting an (often fake) beard and moustache would qualify as … a stranger. Wouldn't you say?

So, don't talk to strangers … but Santa's okay? Hmmm.

Unwanted Touching

Another thing I taught my children, as I think a lot of parents do, is to not let someone touch you if you don't want them to or to tell a parent or safe person if someone does. It could be something relatively innocent like a hug or it could be something worse like molestation. The point is, your body is *your* body and you have a right to say if, when, and who can touch it.

Enter Santa. Not only is he a stranger, but now the parent wants the child to sit on this stranger's lap. The child may "lose it" but only because they are scared (and rightly so given the rules we have taught them). Yet some parents find it funny to subject their children to this.

To me, it seems wrong on so many levels. Forcing your child to sit on a stranger's knee when they clearly are not comfortable doing so.

I never forced my kids to sit on Santa's knee; I would stand with my child beside Santa. We still got a picture with Santa but on terms that were acceptable to both me and my child. If they wanted to sit on Santa's lap when they were older, they could. But I would never force them, and I never will.

I found it ironic that a (seemingly) innocent Facebook post generated more conversation and opinions than something really important like, I don't know, climate change. (Oh wait, some people think that's a myth too.)

Babies Having Babies

When I was in high school, if a girl got pregnant, it was a scandal. At Rivier Academy one of my classmates in Grade 10 wound up pregnant and they kicked her out of school. Granted it was a Catholic school; somehow the standard was higher.

At one of the larger public schools they had a small daycare only teen parents could access. I remember volunteering at lunch time selling popcorn for 50 cents a bag to raise money for the daycare even though I never used it.

I was 19 when I got pregnant with B. The doctor who confirmed I was pregnant asked me if I wanted to keep the child. I had never considered otherwise. Looking back now at the way I was treated by doctors and hospital staff where I gave birth, I recognize I was still considered too young to have a child at that point.

When I was younger, I constantly got ID'ed for cigarettes (which weren't even for me), lottery tickets, and alcohol; I knew better than to purchase any of these items without identification in hand. Where I live, you have to be 18 or 19 to purchase these items.

When B was six, I recall being asked for ID to purchase a lighter at a local store. I looked back and forth between the cashier and my young child. "Really?" I asked, "I would have had to have been 12 when I had my girl."

The cashier dismissed my comment, "Well how did I know she was your daughter?"

To which I replied, "She just called me Mom."

As I shook my head, I handed over my ID.

There is a 14-year gap between B and D. Strangers often assume they are mother and son even though B would have had to have been 14 when she had him. It annoys her when people assume, and she responds (snarkily) that he is her brother.

Times have changed significantly since then. Whether that's good or bad is another question.

B graduated in 2013 from a large, public high school. They had a full class, 35 young women, who already had children. In fact, one had a 4-year-old; which meant she had the baby at 13 or 14!

Having a child when you are that young is hard; I turned 20 shortly after having B and even that was too young. I love my daughter and I don't regret having her; I'm just saying it's hard when you're young and you don't have a support system to help you out. I can't even imagine trying to finish high school while taking care of a child. Parenting is hard work, especially when you are still a child.

Yet somehow, watching these young women cross the stage to get their diplomas brought a (sad) smile to my face because I knew these girls would succeed at whatever they set their minds to. I did.

Pole Dancing

Back before cell phones were quite so popular (yes, there was a time we walked around looking at things in the environment rather than our cell phone screens—shocking, I know), most people would not text and walk at the same time. This has (unfortunately) become the norm now.

B had gotten a cell phone. She was in high school at the time of this incident. She was texting on a non-QWERTY keyboard (you know, the old school keypad with just the numbers on it, where you had to press the same number multiple times depending on which letter you wanted). Anyway, B clearly wasn't paying attention to where she was going because she walked smack-dab into a telephone pole.

After we both stopped laughing, we joked that the pole just appeared out of nowhere. How else do you justify walking into a wooden pole 6-12 inches in diameter and 30+ feet tall?

Zombies

Pokemon Go, a cell phone game, came out a few years back—2015, I think. The objective of the game is to collect virtual critters that wander onto your screen. Usually, people walk around to search for them. If nothing else, it gets people up off their couches and out and about; racking up the steps on their pedometers.

The game is rather unique because you can still see everything on your screen in real life; these little beings just wander into your line of view on your cell phone. So, it's a little different than the previous chapter on pole dancing. But not by much.

You can also battle other people or teams at combat zones. These are set up at random locations. I'm not sure how the game developers decided on the locations of these congregation and/or battle zones. News reports one time remarked on some private home owner who was irked to have one in her yard; she wanted to know how to get off the list, but I don't know if she ever did.

Regina, while it is the second largest city in our province, still numbers a mere 220,000 people. As such, crowds of people could be found swarming around congregation zones.

I admit, I tried it out. For a few weeks. Because I live and work near downtown, I had ample opportunity to find these congregation points—one of which was our downtown library. One nice summer evening, J, D, and I wandered down to the library. The hordes of people wandering around the library was insane! Some people, like me, had given our phones to our children so they could catch these critters. You'd be amazed though at the number of adults participating. As I was watching another parent pushing a stroller, I gazed in awe. He wasn't pushing his child around, so the child could game. No, the parent was playing himself. As he was pushing the stroller. Nudging J, we watched as this man nearly ran his stroller off the sidewalk multiple times (with his child in it)!

J remarked, "Who needs the zombie apocalypse? It's already here," inferring this game was turning people into zombies—real-life, walking, talking, critter-catching zombies.

J gave up the game that night after witnessing this debacle. I played for a few more weeks—until I grew bored with the repetitive tasks. D happily collected them as a passenger in our car—sometimes asking me to stop and wait for him to try to catch one; I had to explain to him I couldn't just slam on the brakes in traffic. Eventually even with D the glossy sheen wore off and he moved on to watching YouTube videos of other people playing games. Yeah, that's a thing apparently.

The zombie apocalypse has indeed arrived. Only it's in the form of cell phones and their (critter-catching) users.

Bedtime Routines

I'm all for routines. We plan our meals at meal times so kids know when they will eat. We plan our days off to make sure we can maximize the number of things we can squeeze into a day. Even on the weekends, when we should be sleeping in, our weekday routines kick in. (Sleeping in for me is 7 a.m.)

We have a bedtime routine. Bath around 6 or 6:30 p.m. Then a story and/or a video on YouTube. By 8 p.m., we're all ready for bed. Kind of.

"Mommy can I have a hug?" or, in our world, "Your arm on me." I co-sleep with my youngest and he seems to need to feel my physical presence with my arm draped over his little body.

"One more (story, video, whatever)." I usually cave but then it's "music time"—when we put on our relaxation tunes and go to sleep.

Sometimes it's about a toy or stuffy that needs to go to bed with us, "Where's Hop or Elly or Mr. Potato Head or Lego guy?" Typically, I don't like to sleep with larger toys in our bed, so I have to convince T to let the toy sleep on the floor. If it's small, it can sleep under his pillow. Unless he's playing with it, then it goes on the floor.

Thankfully I haven't made it to the, "I need a drink of water" or "I have to go potty" stage yet but I'm sure it's coming.

Once we manage to have the lights off, blankets on, videos watched, stories listened to, and toys tucked in we can actually try to sleep. With that 30% of our routine complete, the playing, fooling around, and refusing to sleep starts (not always but often). This uses up the other 70% of our time—where our kids use up every single ounce of our patience and energy. It's why I often end up falling asleep with my kids; I'm just too exhausted to adult any more.

Long gone are the routines where I could get some (much needed) housework done after the little ones go to sleep. Or the hour-long bubble baths I used to be able to enjoy. Or the ability to go out dancing at the clubs. I know it's only temporary and that in a few more years, this period will pass. However, even recognizing that my kids will soon grow up all too fast, there are days where I wish I could have *my* bedtime routine back.

Turn the Television/Computer Off

In this digital age when so many people are hooked to their television and/or computer it becomes difficult to disconnect. I know, personally, I am addicted to electronics. However, one year we decided to travel to Banff. I took my cell phone with me, but I left it turned off unless I needed to make a call. I did not take a laptop. We did not have a television with us. In fact, we did not even rent an electrical stall at the campground. We went camping "old school."

Not only did it ensure I was off my phone, it also forced the teenagers (J's older boys) to disconnect from their phones, which is often very hard. None of us had any problem finding stuff to do on our five-day trip. The teenagers could go for a walk in the morning before the rest of us got out of bed. When we arose, we had breakfast together over a campfire, yes, over a *campfire*. We then would head into town or do some sightseeing. Stopping at the tourist information centre, we picked up maps and ideas of places to visit. We packed lunch before we left as well as snacks. This saved a lot of money considering we had two teenage boys, two adults, and one little boy. It costs a lot to feed a small army!

We made many memories on the trip including seeing a baby bear on the side of the road, a herd of rams in a parking lot, several deer, squirrels that came right up to us, and apparently having two bears walk right through our campground. (Only a thin tent separated us.)

None of these memories could have been made if we had stayed connected to the digital devices we own. So, disconnect and make some new memories.

An Author in Training

"We got two new students in our class today," D stated to me when he came home from Grade 1 one day, "They are from Syria. A lot of their family was killed. Only their mom and dad and them were left alive. They had to leave their home with nothing. That's so sad. They don't even have any toys!"

The conversation turned into a learning experience for my then six-year-old. In his mind, toys were an absolute must. As a middle-income family member, D was fortunate to have pretty much any toy he wanted. They cluttered his room and leaked into other rooms. D took initiative that evening to pack up two boxes of toys to donate to the boys.

Later in the week, D showed me his first written story, complete with hand drawn images entitled "I Love Toys!" It was brilliant! He told me he wanted to publish the book and donate the money to Syrian refugees. We scanned all the pages into the computer—spelling mistakes and all—and uploaded it to the internet. Though it sold no copies, the thought behind it was extraordinary.

My budding author was not concerned with selling his book to make money for himself. He wanted to give his earnings away to other people.

Cat to The Rescue

We wrote a story—J, D and I. Each person wrote a piece—beginning, middle, and end; and somehow, without knowing what the others were writing about, it turned into a real story:

> *Once upon a time, there was a cat that lived in a tree. He was a happy cat. He liked to be in the trees. One day he went camping, then he went back home.*
>
> *Suddenly, a giant dinosaur appeared from a magic vortex right on top of everything! He looked around, jumped up and down, spat 3 times and said, "I am here to deliver a message. If you tell me a secret that no one else knows, I will grant 3 wishes."*

Kitty looked at him, jumped up and down, spat 3 times and said, "I love to hug puppy dogs."

"Woch!" said the dinosaur, "that is an awesome secret. Your wishes are granted.

The next day, the kitty, Bolt, went for a walk to meet his new friends, the ducks.

Huckle, the duck, decided they had learned their lesson and made sure to ask his mom before going down to the lake.

They swam and splashed around. Bolt thanked Huckle for teaching him how to swim. They played all day and stayed the best of friends forever.

The End

Losing J

J and I were only together about five years. In that time, he was a primary guardian for D and a father to my third child, T. J had three kids from a previous marriage who are now in their late teens or early twenties.

He was a great dad; spending time with D and T was what he lived for. He would crawl on the floor with them and sit for hours in a park watching them play. He tried to spend as much time as he could with his older kids as well.

J's diagnosis of colorectal cancer in March 2016 was an absolute shock to everyone in the family. He fought like a trooper; suffering through a round of radiation and multiple bouts of chemotherapy, an ostomy surgery, and then finding out he was terminal—it had spread to his liver and lungs. He tried every alternative treatment we could afford.

In May 2017 after finding out the most recent round of chemo had only shrunk his 5 cm liver tumours by a minute amount and had not touched the multiple smaller tumours in his lungs, he made the very difficult choice to stop treatment. Many long talks had led to the choice of living what time he had left in treatment—feeling nauseous all the time—or just living what time he had left without the nausea. In theory anyway.

Our Last Road Trip

We focused on squeezing in every bit of living we could. I was given the opportunity to take union training in Port Elgin in August 2017; it was Family Education Training and the whole family could attend—J, D, T, and I. Everything was paid for; I took paid vacation from work. Planning to take an extra week after the training to visit a couple water slide parks in Ontario seemed like a good idea. Plans fell together.

The training and vacation were amazing. Despite the constant pain and nausea the cancer brought, J managed to enjoy himself as he watched and played with the boys. He missed a lot of the class because he was so tired, but the instructor understood.

By this time, J could no longer drive because of the medication he was on to control the pain. The Dodge Challenger he had rented us was roomy and decent on gas. We drove from Toronto to Ottawa and went to Calypso Water Park. In the Lazy River ride, J lost his wedding band when it slipped off his finger because of all the weight he had lost. I had a niggly feeling in the back of my mind that this was the universe's way of telling me it was time to start letting go.

We toured the Canadian Mint in Ottawa (something I've always wanted to do) and drove back to Toronto to take in Canada's Wonderland. It was much too crowded for any of us—being from a smaller city of 220,000 people—it felt like all of Regina was crammed into this amusement park. The boys thoroughly enjoyed themselves though and we made lots of memories.

Rapid Decline

J was hospitalized the day after we returned. He was initially told he had a blocked liver duct; they would perform surgery, and all would be good. He would come home during the day time and we thought he would return to the house at some point. Alas, this was not to be.

"Eight weeks," he was told a few days later. He had eight weeks left to live. It turned out the liver duct was blocked by a tumour. It was inoperable. And J had to remain in the hospital, so they could control his pain. I stared at him in shock when he told me. I had no words.

Doctors called a family meeting that week. J's mom, dad, kids, sister, as well as my children and I gathered in the sun room to hear about the course of action. I think we went through their entire supply of Kleenex as the care team told us they would be surprised if J made it *three* more weeks.

Assisted suicide was discussed as an option as it had just become legal. The care team indicated that by the time all the paperwork was done, it would likely be too late. Plus, J had to be of "sound mind" when he made the decision after the paperwork was approved.

Within a week, we went from an operable blocked liver duct to eight weeks down to three weeks.

T was only two at the time. He didn't understand why Daddy couldn't come home. D understood somewhat as he had lost his Nana a couple years prior. B was trying to hold us all together; she became more of a mom to me than I was to her.

We didn't get our three weeks. September 14, 2017, while I was at a hair salon (of all the stupid things), J's mom called to tell me to come to the hospital right away as J was having trouble breathing. As I got into my car, I told J not to wait for me and he didn't. By the time I arrived, not even 10 minutes later, he had died.

Whispers from the Universe

In reflecting on the previous night's visit while sitting in his room waiting for the funeral home to pick up his body, I realized I had known that today would be his last day.

We had taken to having supper together at the hospital—D, T, J, and I (and sometimes others as well). After the family meeting with the doctors, this became a little ritual. By then, J couldn't keep up with T's energy so, after spending half the day with J myself, I brought the boys in to have a (short) supper together in order to limit J's exhaustion.

As J got sicker, he received stronger medication to manage the pain. It made him very sleepy. The night before J passed, he was getting groggy; he faded in and out during this last visit. I have a picture of the boys sitting on the edge of J's hospital bed—eating and watching Paw Patrol on the computer—while J slept (sitting up, with his arms around the boys).

The boys had coloured J some pictures. As I leaned over to tell him I was putting them on his board before we left for the night, J suddenly sat bolt upright, wide awake and said good night to the boys and gave them a (last) hug.

I had an inkling in the back of my mind that would be the last time the boys saw him. The next morning, I purposely did *not* tell the boys we would see J later—something I did every morning since J was hospitalized. I'm glad I didn't because my inkling was right. J always told me to follow my gut and I did.

J's death was hard on us all—not just my little family—but my extended family as well. I cannot count the number of nights the boys and I fell asleep crying. "I miss Daddy too," was our motto for months after J passed.

Providing After Death

Having decided months prior to cremate J's remains, I had purchased a BioUrn to bury J in the back yard under an apple tree. My mom was sick at the time as well and she had decided she wanted the same thing. You see, apple trees require at least two to be planted within 50 feet of each other to cross-pollinate. Mom's tree would cross pollinate with J's tree and that way they both could continue providing for the family after death. I know that's kind of corny but that's the kind of person J was—always putting his family first.

Having two apple trees to cross pollinate came to fruition a mere 11 days after we lost J; my mom succumbed to COPD (Chronic Obstructive Pulmonary Disease—lung disease/failure) and was cremated as well. Now I was left planning a second funeral the same month.

My brother had travelled from Alberta to Regina for the funerals. He dug the holes for the urns and apple trees. The ashes of J and my mom were each put in a BioUrn; these urns sat on the picnic table while my brother dug the holes. T walked over and asked me, "What's this?" while pointing at his dad's BioUrn. I told him it was Daddy. T picked up the urn carefully and gently gave it a kiss and a hug. I cried. With the kids' help, we placed the urns in their respective holes and planted the trees on top.

This spring, we dubbed the trees Daddy's tree and Gramma's tree. They get hugs from time to time. Though I have to be careful with T around; I can't call it Gramma's tree—to him it's *my* mom's tree. He knows J's mom as Gramma and she is very much with us (hopefully for a long time to come).

We had no apples this year, but similar to grieving, apple trees take years to bear fruit. The fruit will come as the years pass; by then maybe our loss will be less raw.

Potty-Training

With my oldest child, the daycare did most of the potty-training for me. I just had to reinforce it at home.

Accidents happened. I knew getting upset at accidents would set back potty-training efforts, so I tried to be as calm as possible. One of the things I had B do when she had an accident was to change her sheets. Even if it was in the middle of the night. Of course, I helped her. It was not a punishment to me, it was a natural consequence.

My middle son was also at daycare during those potty-training years. One day he came home from daycare in his pullups, quite proud he was wearing "big boy underwear." I chucked softly as I explained that "big boy underwear" was actual underwear (which I had on hand to show him) not a pullup. That day, he decided that's what he wanted to wear and that was the end of diapers for him. Just like that.

T, my youngest, seems to be a bit more challenging. He is at daycare and he does well when he is there. As soon as he gets home, he forgets all about using the potty. His dad, before he passed, bought him a potty that made music when you peed into it. That lasted a couple of weeks until T decided he was scared of it. Frankly, I don't blame him. I don't like my toilet to make noise when I pee in it either. Don't even get me started on those auto-flush toilets.

Gramma suggested a potty seat that fit on the big toilet. I found one on VarageSale—it's even got Paw Patrol on it. The challenge, however, continues. We tried peeing on Cheerios; that worked for just over a week. I've tried the reward system with stickers. I've tried bribing. He just turned three and we're still working on it.

He has started telling me when he has to poop. However, he tells me as he is going to squat and hide to do the deed. Usually between the couch and the cat tree where no one can see him. One evening (before he turned three), when Gramma was over, we had his diaper off because it was chafing. Gramma was texting, and I was playing a game on my phone. We heard T exclaim, "I pooped!"

Gramma and I looked up at him and one of us asked, "You have to go poop?"

"No, I pooped!" he repeated as he pointed at the floor by my feet.

Right beside me, a two-inch log lay on the carpet. Gramma and I looked at each other as we cracked up laughing. She rushed him to the potty to finish and I grabbed some tissue to pick the poop up and dispose of it.

Ah, the joys of potty-training.

Gas

Toddlers learn new words and infer their meaning. T knows burping is when gas noisily comes out of your mouth. It only makes sense then that gas noisily coming out of your other end is burping, as in "Burping out my butt."

Graffiti

Graffiti is prevalent in many of the neighbourhoods I have lived in. My kids and I sometimes discuss why people do this. Especially after our garage had been "tagged." I have made D promise never to deface (or damage or steal) other people's property because those people work hard for the things they have and it's annoying (and expensive) to remove or replace it.

Apparently, though, this does not apply to our own stuff. LOL! B was about nine or ten when she decided to write on the back seat of our car with a black marker. My ex hubby and I were quite disappointed. We used the opportunity to teach B about why we don't do these things and she helped clean it off. Thankfully, it was a dark seat, so it didn't show too much.

Stupid Ads (YouTube)

I saw a post on Facebook the other day that stated,

> *"I feel sorry for Netflix era kids. They will never know the high stakes adrenaline of running to the bathroom/fridge/bedroom in a single ad break, with the beckoning call of a sibling screaming, "It's ONNNNNN" to send you hurdling over furniture to get back in time"*—Felicity @FlossAus

My generation can relate to this; I remember trying to get a snack ready in the kitchen during the commercials or making bathroom runs. Then rushing back to watch the show. Depending on the show, we had two to four minutes. We even timed the first few commercials during a show to know how much time we had and adjust our tasks accordingly.

T watches YouTube; when ads come on now, he growls, "Stupid ads!" These ads are short—less than thirty seconds in total. He knows how to skip them if they're a little longer. When I was little, ads used 1/3 of the show's time. A thirty-minute show could be watched in twenty minutes without the ads (if you had a DVR or PVR, you could skip ads completely when they came on).

The struggle is real. Yes, I know, first world problems. On the positive side, there is a pause button on YouTube when you have to go do something and you can skip the majority of the ad if you desire.

The (Power) Struggle is Real

Another struggle that is real, aside from "stupid ads," is power struggles. Usually these are between parent and child. B used to say, "What-e-ver!" while sashaying her hand in front of her face. D rolls his eyes or glares at you. T cries, yells, or throws stuff (sometimes all three at once).

I have learned, through my wonderful parenting course, that these power struggles happen because we are ordering, correcting, and directing our kids (staying in the Parent Ego State) too much. Our actions as parents strip our children of their power and so they seek power in any other way they can—for example by pushing back (yelling, throwing stuff), pushing our buttons (whining), rolling their eyes/glaring, and/or backtalking. ("What-ever!")

Small choices give your children back their power. Choices like bath or shower; jeans or sweats; green or red jello; ice cream cone or creamsicle; apple or orange; time out or meditation; blue soap or red. These little choices fill your child's power bucket and will thus reduce these power struggles. Offer a choice when you can; the difference you see in your kids will be a-maz-ing.

Ghosts

We have a ghost. His name is Steve. He's not malicious but he does like to hide things. I've lost things for days or weeks; spent time scouring the house—eventually to find the item in plain sight at a later date. Lego men my daughter and I searched for that appeared an hour later on an end table we both searched. Multiple times. I've found credit cards and wallets in the freezer. (Talk about cold, hard cash.) While you might chalk this up to not looking properly, I know for a fact (okay, maybe not a scientific fact) that ghosts exist. I've had too many unexplained life events happen to me.

I'm digressing again, sorry. When you have kids, things get misplaced. It could be an absent-minded accident like when I put B's antibiotics in the china cabinet instead of the fridge. Or it could be someone just forgot where they put it. The latter is probably the actual truth. I prefer to blame it on Steve, though.

Present Moment Mindfulness

One of my late hubby's favourite TV shows was "Dead Like Me." The main character was a young girl whose life is terminated unexpectedly when she is struck on the head by a rogue toilet seat that fell from the space station. J often said cancer was his proverbial toilet seat.

If I have learned anything over the last couple of years, it's that life is way too short and we really need to focus on living for today. What does that mean? To me, that means living life in the present; focusing on making memories; and appreciating joyful moments. Today I'm going to share one story for each of these three life lessons.

A friend of mine was lamenting her current relationship. She did not have confidence in where it was heading. Questioning where the relationship would be in five years, she felt her boyfriend did not have a long-term vision for them. This was when J was still in treatment but had not been diagnosed with Stage 4 cancer (it was not terminal at this point).

I asked her, "Are you happy?"

With a quizzical expression on her face, she paused and quietly asked, "What?"

"Right now, are you happy with your relationship?" I asked.

She replied, "Yes."

"Then don't worry about five years down the road. Who knows what will happen in the next five years? You may not be alive. J and I planned to bring up our children and grow old together. Cancer threw a wrench in that plan."

Lesson #1—Live life in the present.

Fast forward a few months later to when J was diagnosed as Stage 4 (it was terminal). I had another friend who had come into a bit of money and was feeling guilty about spending it on a family trip to Disneyland rather than doing the "practical" thing and paying down her mortgage. I told her I thought it was a great idea! What a fabulous way to make memories with her husband and children! *That* is what life should be about. *That* is what will keep her kids going after she has left this world. Not that the bills were paid or the mortgage was clear. These memories would be priceless to them.

Lesson #2—Focus on making memories.

Fast forward again to after J had passed. I was sitting at home one day shortly after J's death, absentmindedly watching my boys who were two and eight at the time. I was not really paying attention to anything. Zoned out, so to speak. Suddenly, I stopped and really focused on them. Here they were banging their little toys together, laughing and giggling; living right there in the moment. Cares left by the wayside. Joy radiating from their beautiful little faces.

Lesson #3—Appreciate joyful moments.

We always thought we had more time. People often take the time we have for granted, postponing their dreams and desires to "some time later." Some of us lose out on our hopes and dreams because of our own deliberate inaction and some because fate has other plans. I call it living for today; J would have called it "present moment mindfulness." Either way, the lessons remain the same:

- ∞ Live life in the present.
- ∞ Focus on making memories.
- ∞ Appreciate joyful moments.

I want to encourage all of you to take these lessons to heart. Now. Before you get hit on the head with your proverbial toilet seat. Namaste.

Cheerleading and 6-packs

Before we had the either of the boys, my ex-husband and I were on a shopping trip at the local grocery store with B. She had just started Grade 9. While we were in the lineup, B was telling me about the various things they were doing in cheerleading. At one point, as she pulled up her shirt a little way, she excitedly stated, "Look, I even have 6-pack abs!"

Chuckling, my ex replied, "So do I, they are just under a layer of fat." The gentleman behind us tried, unsuccessfully, to hold back a laugh. Sometimes you just have to look at the humour in life.

When my daughter told me she enrolled in cheerleading, I have to admit I was thoroughly disenchanted. Although I never was around cheerleaders in my high school, I definitely had some preconceived notions about them. Notions fed from movies and media. I was judgmental. I thought cheerleading was one of those girly activities where young women wore skimpy outfits to attract attention. And so, I struggled with her choice to join cheerleading.

Skimpy outfits aside, I quickly learned cheerleading is not a girly activity; some boys were even on the cheerleading team. In fact, cheerleading is a sport which requires a lot of strength, a lot of discipline, and a lot of coordination.

My daughter was a "base;" this means she had the responsibility of throwing and catching the person that was being tossed up in the air (the "flyer"). Usually, there were three "bases." Often, she came home with bruises. On one particular day, she had more than usual. When I inquired about them, she explained two of the "bases" had stepped back after tossing the "flyer" up in the air. The "flyer" had launched wrong and was coming down in an awkward position. B had to catch the "flyer" on her own. The "flyer" landed right on top of B. If B hadn't stepped up to be a human mat, the "flyer" would have dropped 6-12 feet onto the cement floor—resulting in broken bones, not just bruises. Afterwards, the coach drove home the point to the other two "bases" that it was imperative for them to catch the "flyer" *no matter what*.

I also remember a time when B came home from high school and told me the football players (the big, strong football players) were heckling them that cheerleading wasn't a real sport, so the girls invited the boys to be the "bases" for the "flyers." I think that really opened the boys' eyes because none of the football players ever heckled the cheerleaders again that year.

Cheerleading can be quite competitive as well; an aspect I wasn't aware of in the beginning. I thought it was just something that was done at the school. How very wrong I was. (See, I'm *still* not afraid to admit I was wrong.) Many of the city schools compete in professional cheerleading competitions; pom, stunt, team and otherwise.

I didn't always agree with the choices my daughter made as a high school student. But it definitely opened my eyes to what being a good parent was. Just because *I* didn't like sports and *I* didn't like cheerleading (because of the way the media portrayed cheerleaders) didn't mean my daughter had to dislike the same things. She chose to be a cheerleader. And I'm so very glad she did. It made me realize that even though my daughter was growing up to have different likes and dislikes, she was growing up making those choices for herself. I tried not to press her to do what I wanted. I let her make that choice for herself and I will continue to let my boys make choices for themselves as they grow up. Because I really, truly believe one of the best things a parent can do for their children is to let them be themselves and not try to dictate their life for them.

Adulting

"Don't make me adult today; I can't adult today." Some variation of this quote is often circulated on Facebook. Someone was wearing a T-shirt with this slogan the other day. I smile whenever I see the quote. With all the emotional ups and downs associated with being a parent, there are days when I truly do not want to "adult."

I used to joke that there were days when I just wanted to walk away; to be free of taking care of another human being; to live my life for myself instead of always putting my kids first.

Then my sister-in-law decided she didn't want to be a wife and mom of three anymore. One day, at the Calgary Zoo, during a family outing, she texted my brother and told him she was done being a mom. He went out to talk to her in the parking lot and afterwards, she hopped on the C-Train—leaving my brother as a single dad with three small children under the age of ten. She never did go back to them.

After that incident, I could no longer joke about leaving my family; it was no longer a joking matter to me. I still think about the "what ifs" from time to time but I push the thoughts aside and I definitely don't vocalize them anymore.

On a serious note, if you are having thoughts of harming or leaving your children, please seek help immediately. Talk to your family doctor or another health specialist. It's important to address these thoughts before you do something drastic that could affect you, your children and/or your spouse in such a negative manner. You may not want to "adult," but you have a responsibility to do so.

Teaching Me

Focusing on my children has helped me move through the grief of losing my partner (and my mom shortly after). I have no doubt if I did not have those little bodies to feed and take care of, I wouldn't have gotten out of bed for weeks after J passed. But these boys are resilient; they grieve but then they go back to life. They are sad inside and then they put on a happy face and play.

I think it's harder for adults. Maybe we've lost some of the joy that should motivate us. I'm thankful I have my children (most days anyway). They teach me so much. Whether it's to stop and chase "Hop" or to test my patience, there is something to be learned from these wonderful little beings.

I was having a moment one morning; I was missing J something fierce. They say healing takes time. It's been almost a year and I still have moments. One morning, I was sitting on the end of my bed crying. I had left the children in the living room with their toys, so I could have some privacy.

It was one of those days when I didn't want to "adult." I was struggling with everything going on in life at the moment. T who was two at the time, came into the room and just watched me. He knew something was wrong. I told him I was good and to go play. He came over to me, put his little, precious hand on me and said, "I love you Mommy."

I smiled at him and replied (half laughing, half crying), "I love you too. Let's go get your breakfast." I wiped my tears and continued adulting.

Sometimes I wait until the children are in bed before I let myself cry. I mean really cry. One night I thought T was asleep and I was softly sobbing in bed beside him. He stirred and called out to me. I replied I was fine. "I just miss Daddy," I said.

"I miss Daddy too," he replied.

We cried ourselves to sleep that night; T kept saying, "I miss Daddy too."

Whenever he saw me sad over the next few weeks, he would softly whisper our own private mantra, "I miss Daddy too." And I would give him a hug and try to smile.

Showing emotion to our children is not a bad thing. I have realized my boys are, in their own way, teaching me how to show my emotion more and to allow them to grieve as well.

Just because they seem to be holding it all together, they remember their missing loved one(s); they need to grieve too.

Generational Gap — Definition of Sexy

I remember my mom telling me one time how she thought Tom Selleck was sexy. As a teenager, the appeal of a dark, filled-in moustache escaped my definition of attractive. Despite both of my husbands having facial hair, I still find men better looking without the beard and/or moustache. (Usually, but not always.)

Fast forward to 2012. Magic Mike, a movie about male strippers, was in the theatres and despite my better judgement I kind of wanted to see it. So, when my daughter suggested it as a mother-daughter date, I agreed. Both of us agreed we wanted to see the movie for its eye candy and we each drooled a bit when we spoke the names of the male actor we found most sexy. At the same time, I said "Matthew McConaughey" and B said "Channing Tatum." We looked at each other and exclaimed, "Ew!" to the other person's choice and burst out laughing.

Clearly, there *is* a generational gap in the definition of sexy.

To Moustache or Not to Moustache

My ex had a moustache almost the entire time I met him. He kept it well trimmed. I admit, it suited him.

When B was around age 3, my ex decided he was going to shave it off. He sat B on the toilet (with the lid closed) while he took out the shaving cream, applied it, and shaved the moustache off completely.

B watched in fascination. When he was done, he looked over at her; she giggled and exclaimed, "Put it back on Daddy!"

Since then, my ex has honoured B's wishes and kept the moustache.

Money

When I was younger if I wanted to have some spending money, I had to do chores in the neighbourhood. For example, I used to rake the neighbor's yards. Usually I charged $2 per yard (front or back) and an extra $1 if they had something gross (like dog poo) to clean up. One older lady down the street from us would hire my brother and I every year to rake her front and back yards. Because her back yard had crabapples rotting on the ground, we got paid $5 for the whole job. This was a windfall for us.

Sometimes if business was slow and we wanted something small, we would only charge 50 cents. On one of those occasions, we offered to rake a lady's back yard for this super low rate. She was kind enough to not only hire us but to pay us $2 each *and* gave us both a bottle of pop. (Pik-a-Pop if you remember that.) Back then a bottle of pop was a huge treat; and back then, $1 could buy a lot more candy than it does now. In fact, you could buy one cent candies at the local convenience store and because there was no tax back then, $1 actually bought 100 candies. Candy was eaten a lot less frequently than it is today; it was a real treat.

Squeegee Kids

Sometimes in the city I currently live in, there are young teenagers who will stand at street corners with a squeegee in their hands (dubbed "squeegee kids"). When the traffic light turns red, they will run out into the stopped traffic and squeegee someone's windshield with hopes that person will feel guilty and give money to them. Even though I know they're just trying to make money in the way they know how, I always wave them away because I feel like they should be asking permission before just going ahead and squeegeeing your window then expecting payment from you.

One day, I used this as a teaching opportunity for my daughter (who was quite a bit younger than she is now). After explaining about various social programs that were available to people, I told her if she was ever *that* desperate for money, she could always call me. I tried to reiterate the fact that if she was ever short money and felt she needed to do something she didn't want to do like begging for money, there were alternatives and that my door would always be open; I would help her however I could.

I try to do the same thing with my boys as they grow up; I will continue to reinforce the idea that, while I won't necessarily give them *everything* that they want money wise, I will definitely make sure they have their basic needs met and they don't have to resort to begging other people for money.

Paying for Chores

When I was a lot younger, I used to think giving an allowance was a good idea and I tied the allowance to chores. Recently however, I have taken the chores part and separated it from the allowance. In fact, I really try to refer to chores as household contributions (as the parenting course I am taking encourages).

Allowance payment is made by auto debit from my account into each of the boys' accounts. While recognizing the importance of teaching children to actually go to the bank, everything is becoming more automated; it's likely there will not be banks in the near future (at least not for depositing money). For now, money accumulates in their bank accounts. When there is a big purchase they want to make for themselves (like a tablet), they can pay for it out of their accounts.

Stuff

Another thing I struggle with is buying the boys all the "stuff" they want. Because we're such a materialistic society, I often find it difficult when we go on a shopping trip and my boys expect a new toy. I suppose it doesn't help when restaurants like McDonald's give a toy with every Happy Meal. This inadvertently becomes something expected—even if it is just a small item that usually ends up in the trash shortly after coming home.

In order to help combat some of this materialism (and the clutter it brings), I try to make a rule that when a new toy comes home, another toy gets donated to someone less fortunate. That, however, doesn't always work out. Instead I find myself going through toys (when the boys are not around)—throwing out the broken ones and donating the ones that are still usable (but the boys have outgrown or no longer play with).

Instilling in my children the fact that not everyone is fortunate as they are is important to me. D was in Grade 1 when there was the Syrian crisis and a lot of Syrian refugees were relocating to Canada. Earlier in this book, I explained how D came home from school one day to relay to me there were some new boys in his class—refugees who had to leave all their family behind except their mom, dad, and each other. His realization that they didn't even get to bring their toys with them was a really big thing for him. He kept reiterating the story to me. I used it as a learning opportunity to educate him there were people who didn't have anything. And you may recall my sweet, beautiful, considerate boy went into his room and packed up a couple boxes of toys to take to his new friends. My heart still swells with pride at his action.

Financial Know How

No one ever taught me about money. No one ever taught me about investing or saving money from my paycheck. These were all new concepts to me and, as a young adult, I wasn't well versed in the financial well-being of my family. We lived paycheck to paycheck. It's only recently, with the loss of my husband, I have been able to have an extra pool of money in case of emergencies.

My hope is to integrate financial know how into my children's skill set. To ensure they are well off financially while still realizing there are others less fortunate and we, as a society, need to help them.

Contributing to society as a middle-class family and paying taxes are some of the things we do to help support social programs; some of which I have used in the past. I've been on both ends of the spectrum as far as living on minimum wage back in 1993 when I graduated from high school. I've lived paycheck to paycheck. I know the pains of having your car break down in between paychecks or even on payday when the money has already been allotted (and needing to redistribute the money from one necessity to another). I've lived on Social Services. I've lived on student loans (which is pretty much like Social Services because you really don't have any extra money to spend). Savings were unheard of. If you missed work, there were no sick days—you were out that day's pay.

Now that I'm self-sufficient and my income is enough to cover all of the necessities of myself and my household, I realize how far I've come. Teaching my children financial knowledge is crucial for me. They currently each have a savings account which I contribute to regularly.

I think it's the responsibility of every parent out there to make sure their children are informed about their financial responsibilities and, while I know nine years old (or younger) is probably too young to grasp the concepts of debits and credits, we can at least start the savings mindset early.

Our education system fails our children in the area of financial know how. It's simply not taught in elementary or secondary school how to create and/or live on a budget or to save and/or invest. These are critical skills everyone should learn. Schools aren't teaching our children so it's up to the parents. I encourage each of you to foster this knowledge in your kids; teach them the value of money. Teach them to be compassionate, knowledgeable, fully functioning adults within our society.

Money may not buy happiness, but it definitely helps (by alleviating anxiety).

An Average Day in the Life of a Parent

Parenting is exhausting. Period. Let's quickly review an average day in *my* life as a parent; as you recognize the drudgery and repetition that goes along with it, be thankful you have not (completely) lost your mind.

My first weekday alarm rings at 5:30 a.m. Most days, I simply can't bring myself to get up this early. So, I turn it off and doze again for 30 minutes until my second alarm goes off at 6:00 a.m. Then I must get up if I have *any* hope at all of getting to work on time.

Several failed attempts later at nagging the boys to get out of bed (which, ironically, they have no problem doing on the weekend—without any encouragement), we sit down to breakfast. Between mouthfuls, both boys stare mindlessly at a random cartoon playing on YouTube like they've never seen anything like it before.

After that we get dressed. Well, we try. But my three-year-old is fussy; sometimes he doesn't want to wear his diaper/pants/shirt because "they hurt," or "he's scared." (Notice I didn't mention socks here? More about that shortly.) By the time I have the youngest child (and myself) dressed, my older child (currently nine) has effectively procrastinated sufficiently to have done precisely bupkiss (except boring a mental hole in the wall from staring so hard). A quick holler at him and I discover he has "no clean pants." I swear softly under my breath (well, loud enough for anyone in the house to hear—let's be honest) as I march into his room (we all know how children look for stuff with their eyes closed) to find his "missing" pants which usually end up being in his drawer or the clean laundry basket I asked him to put away the weekend before. Sometimes he will protest "he doesn't wear jeans" or he doesn't like those particular ones for some silly reason or another. Eventually, he too gets dressed.

I like to be ready to head out the door by 7:15 a.m. However, with two small children it's usually 7:30 a.m. or later. We finally get to the back door—almost ready to leave. Cue the "leaving the house" tantrum from the younger boy.

Either the socks or the shoes "hurt." Note that the socks in question are the only kind he will wear because everything else has seams in them which rub his feet wrong (subsequently "hurting" his poor sensitive feet). The ones he likes, in other words. As I pull the sock and shoe on the second foot, the other one is ripped off and thrown. Some mornings, it's not worth the argument so I just grab him, the socks and shoes, and carry him out to the car. By the time we get to daycare, he is (finally) ready to put them on.

Jackets are a whole nother beast. Both my children refuse to wear them unless it's frigid outside. People look at *me* funny when it's cold out and the boys aren't properly dressed. I just shrug it off.

Now it's probably 7:40 a.m. by the time I pull up to the daycare to drop off the boys. They are on separate floors, so this takes 10-15 minutes. And then I have 5-10 minutes to get to work.

I spend the next nine hours sitting at my desk putting fires out (figuratively speaking). I'm in IT so these are usually of a technical nature. I get an hour lunch break (which I utilize for several other tasks that need to get done, like writing and Toastmasters). Then at 4:47 p.m. I fight traffic to pick up the boys and head home.

By then it's supper time so I either cook or have grabbed something from a fast food joint on the way home (don't you wiggle your pointer finger at me). We eat in relative peace (either on the couch or in front of the TV or computer).

Bath time! Most times, there are more toys in the tub than room for people. Sometimes it's the boys together but more often it's me and my youngest, then D afterwards.

That leaves us time to play a bit, read, or watch YouTube cartoons. The boys are in bed by 8 p.m. most nights.

Sometimes I fall asleep at the same time as the boys, leaving me no time for myself (hence why I bathe with T).

The next morning, we rinse and repeat the same routine—all week long. No time for much else.

Here's a quick footnote. I live within a 12-block radius of work and daycare; I should be able to walk the boys to daycare and get back to work with ease. Furthermore, I *should* be able to walk *and* save the $14/day parking fee at the mall parking lot. However, this never seems to happen. I tried. It added an hour each way and that's precious time I don't have in the day.

We have a routine now. A monotonous one but it took a year to get to this point—where I can (almost) get to work every day on time. Maybe next year I'll be able to establish a new routine that involves walking and saving money on parking. Okay, let's be realistic … probably not.

It's Okay to Not Be Okay

Over the last couple of years, I have decided it's okay to not be okay. Life takes us in different directions than what we planned sometimes. Being a parent is a really hard job. It's a 24 hour, sometimes messy, sometimes thankless, all-consuming job. Some days it is rewarding and others, it's just plain exhausting.

It has been just over a year since I lost J (and my mom). My boys have kept me functioning through the grief. Some days it's three steps forward and two steps back but I'm still moving forward. Most days anyway. I still have good days and bad.

Some days the kids seem to know not only how to push my buttons but how to slam their hands down on the keyboard all at once. And then in the next moment they are snuggling up to me, reliving their day, telling me how I'm their "best friend." They struggle too. Sometimes I forget that.

It's taken me 12 full months to adjust to our new "normal." Our new routines that focus on the boys' and my well-being. I'm not perfect; I never claimed to be. I am doing the best I can with what I have. And it's hard sometimes. So very hard.

Today I had another bout with my failure as a parent after I lost my patience with T's whining; it brought me to tears afterwards and I could not face work, so I stayed home and watched Netflix (and wrote a couple chapters).

I try to remember that in writing this book, I've come up with more positives than negatives and that makes me smile. It's okay to not be okay. And I've decided I'm okay with that.

Summary

We've been through rough roads, potholes and severe swerving, onto a smoother road where things went better than planned then through stormy weather with patches of sunshine. The Path to Perfection, obviously, isn't smooth and carefree; it takes work to navigate.

Regardless of how hard we try, how many books we read, how much advice we solicit—there really is no way to be a perfect parent. Parents are not supplied a "how to" guide at the birth of their child(ren).

At times I wish there *was* a roadmap that provided us all the instruction we needed to become a perfect parent. Something we could follow step by step; and it would lead us to this place of parental perfection. Alas, there isn't. We're all wired differently; we improvise along the way. Sometimes things go well and sometimes they don't.

The journey itself is the map; we create it on the fly as we go. We do the best we can with what we have. Somehow the kids turn into intelligent, caring, and thoughtful adults who will follow their own intuition and strive to be the same (non) perfect parents.

One Foot Forward

Losing a partner. If not for my kids needing me to get them ready every day, I have no doubt I would have stayed in bed most days. I would have taken much more leave from work. I would have sunk into more of a depression than I did. I still have my ups and downs; good days and bad. For the most part, I keep moving forward. It's slow. I slide back some days. Especially when T says, "I miss Daddy." Yeah, I miss him too. I will forever. To infinity and beyond, "equal."

One foot forward, day by day—that's how you move on after losing someone.

Summary

If I Could Do It Again ...

I would do it all the same.

I'm totally kidding. I would do a lot of the things the same, but I would definitely do some things differently. You know what though? I'd probably still do something "wrong" in someone's eyes; someone would still pass judgment on me—heck, I would pass judgment on me. No matter how many times I changed it up, I would probably still find other examples of things I could have done differently. Like a speech you keep refining that is never quite perfect or a craft you made a mistake on that only you can see.

So, take it easy on yourself Momma (or Papa), you're doing stuff right.

Reaching Perfection

Remember that golden destination we envisioned at the beginning of this book? Perfection; your target destination as a parent. Remember that road or path we were on with the one, clearly marked, exit? The one where you would end up in Perfection with all the other perfect parents?

Prior to writing this book, I contemplated if Perfection existed at all; essentially, the exit would lead to nowhere. In the beginning of this book, I assumed this location *did* exist. However, I hypothesized that if any parent actually made it to Perfection they would find it empty because all the other parents would have been waylaid along the path, thus never reaching their destination. Perfection would be a very lonely place for anyone who ever made it there.

Now I think I must reconsider my own hypothesis. Perfection exists. It's not a lonely place. However, there is not just one exit; there are an infinite number of exits leading to Perfection. Regardless of which path you take, you will reach your destination eventually.

To all those parents reading this book, you *are* on your way to Perfection (or maybe you've already reached it). Keep up the awesome work!

Final Words

In finishing this book, I was overjoyed to realize I had more examples of things I did "right" than things I did "wrong." I guess it turns out that even though I'm not a perfect parent, I'm not a horrible one, either.

I'm going to refer back to the poem I quoted in the beginning and focus on one part:

> *Those little eyes that look up at you—they think you are perfect. They think you are more than enough.*
>
> *Those little hands that reach out to hold you—they think you are the strongest. They think you can conquer the world.*
>
> *Those little mouths eating the food you gave them—they think that you are the best because their bellies are full.*
>
> *Those little hearts that reach out to touch yours—they don't want anything more. They just want you.*

I'm *not* the perfect parent. I never professed to be. And I never will be. My kids think I'm perfect though and *that* is good enough for me.

About the Author

Dawn Thomas-Cameron is a parent and full-time breadwinner for her family. In her "real" life, Dawn works in Information Technology as a Systems Analyst (like a Programmer but with more meetings). She holds a Bachelor of Science in Computer Science from the University of Saskatchewan. She currently resides in Regina, Saskatchewan (Canada) with her children.

As a (non) perfect parent of three children ranging in age from three years to 23 years, Dawn is still continuing her journey along her Path to Perfection. With such a variety of ages in her children, Dawn's parenting method morphed and changed over time. There are no official awards for being a parent; but the unofficial ones are plentiful–like watching your children grow into responsible, caring, empathetic adults.

Editor of The Art of Being Alive (written by her late husband, Jason Cameron), Dawn has written various short stories, articles, blog articles and is currently the editor of The Busy Signal, Unifor Local 1-S's newsletter. She won an award with Young People's Press for her short story, Fleeing Gerald.

This book (the first—and assuredly not the last—Dawn has published) is the culmination of 23 years of experience as a parent, experience in communication and leadership skills (courtesy Toastmasters) and past writing on a variety of topics.

http://www.thepathtoperfection.com/
https://windingrants.wordpress.com/

CPSIA information can be obtained
at www.ICGtesting.com
Printed in the USA
LVHW030121240919
631984LV00019B/1116/P